# Sharpen Up!

## New York
## English Language Arts

BOOK 8

**Buckle Down**
PUBLISHING COMPANY

## ACKNOWLEDGMENTS:

Intermediate Learning Standards from the University of the State of New York, the State Education Department. Used with permission.

Excerpt from *Life on the Mississippi* by Mark Twain. Public domain.

Excerpt from "The Moustache" by Robert Cormier. From *Eight Plus One* by Robert Cormier. Copyright © 1975 by Robert Cormier. Reprinted by permission of Pantheon Books, a division of Random House, Inc.

Excerpt from *The Great Flood of '55* by Tom Fitzpatrick. Copyright © 1990 by Rick Zollo. Reprinted by permission of the author.

Excerpt from "To Build a Fire" from *Lost Face* by Jack London. Public domain.

"The Old Spotted Dog" from *The Autobiography of Will Rogers*, selected and edited by Donald Day, with a foreword by Bill and Jim Rogers. Copyright © 1949 by the Rogers Company. Reprinted with permission of The Will Rogers Memorial Commission.

"Slom Season" adapted from *Mårbacka: The Story of a Manor* by Selma Lagerlöf. Public domain.

Excerpt from *The Mysterious Island* by Jules Verne. Public domain.

"A Patch of Old Snow" from *Mountain Interval* by Robert Frost. Public domain.

ISBN 0-7836-1802-6

Catalog #SU NY8E 1

7 8 9 10

President and Publisher: Douglas J. Paul, Ph.D.; Editorial Director: John Hansen; Senior Editor: Karen Nichols; Editors: Greta Anderson, James A. Bartlett, Ted Remington, Julia Wasson Render, Rick Zollo; Production Director: Jennifer Booth; Art Director: Chris Wolf.

Cover: Images © 1996 PhotoDisc, Inc.

# TABLE OF CONTENTS

# Introduction

This book has been written to help you prepare for the Grade 8 New York English Language Arts Test. It contains a review of the basic language arts skills outlined by the state. These skills will help you with reading throughout your school career and beyond.

This book also contains test-taking tips. These tips will help you understand the test-taking process and do your personal best on test day.

## What's on the Test?

The test will measure your skills in reading, listening, and writing. You will read several selections—fiction (made-up stories), nonfiction (selections about real people, places, events, or ideas), and poetry. You also will listen to one or more selections read aloud to you. Then, you will answer questions about what you have read or heard. Some questions will be of the multiple-choice variety; others will require you to write your response.

## You Can Do It (with a Little Motivation and Practice)

Your reading skills will play an important part in your success on the state test. One of the best ways you can prepare for the test is to read—a lot.

Everybody is interested in *something,* but we're not all interested in the *same* things. Our motivation to read depends a great deal on our interest in the subject matter.

For example, let's say that you don't know anything about how cars work. If a copy of *Basic Car Mechanics* landed on your desk, you might say, "I can't possibly read this stuff. It's too hard."

Then, the summer before you turn 16, your Aunt Matilda gives you a surprise. She takes you to the old garage where her 1966 Mustang convertible sits in storage. "It's yours," she says, "if you can get it to run." Suddenly, you have a "driving" interest in *Basic Car Mechanics.* You also start reading magazines like *Collector Cars* and keep a copy of *Chilton's Ford Mustang Repair Manual* under your pillow. Who would have guessed your reading would achieve that kind of horsepower?

Maybe cars aren't your thing. But *something* is. If you want to become a better reader, your first job is to find out what your interests are. Then read all you can about those topics. Immerse yourself in something that is fascinating to you, *whatever* it is.

The point is this: Reading is easy if you want to do it. It doesn't matter so much *what* you choose to read, just that you *read.* The more you read, the easier reading will become.

# General Tips for Taking Language Arts Tests

The people who do best on tests approach them as if they were a game. Natural ability helps, but you can go far if you've put in the practice, have a sound "game plan," and are able to concentrate on the day of the test.

Here are some general tips to think about as you practice:

### Do a "first read" of the selection.

The first time you read a selection, read to discover, not to take in every last word. Find out what the selection is *mainly* about. Don't concern yourself with every detail or get hung up on words you don't know. Just try to get a feel for the basic concepts. It also helps to keep a "map" in your head of where concepts are mentioned in the selection.

If you need to, slow down and go back over a difficult idea. But don't stop. Keep moving until you come to the end of the selection.

### Learn how to answer the different question types.

Each lesson in this book explains a type of question that is likely to appear on the test and gives you tips on how to answer it.

### Base your answers only on what is in the selection.

You're being tested on how well you read, not on how much you know about the topic of the selection. In all but a few cases, don't use outside knowledge to answer the reading questions. Base your answers on the information given to you in the selection.

### Read each question carefully.

Make sure you understand each question before you select your answer. Don't jump ahead and select an answer before you've read the entire question and *all* the answer choices.

## "Skim" the selection for the correct answer.

Skimming is an important skill, but you need to know when to use it. Don't skim the first time through. After you've read the entire selection and feel you've understood it, the best way to find an answer usually is to skim to find key words. You will learn more about skimming in Lesson 2.

## Don't leave any blanks.

Even if you aren't sure of an answer, you should always make your best guess. By answering, you at least have a chance to get the question right. *Not* answering a question is a guaranteed miss.

*Before* you guess, always eliminate answers that seem as if they are probably wrong. Your odds of answering correctly will be improved if you do.

## On test day, relax.

If you've practiced the material in this book, your new skills will be "built-in" by test day. You won't be worried because you'll know that you can do your best.

# unit 1

## In This Unit

Main Idea and Theme

Details and Sequencing of Events

Vocabulary in Context

Visual Information Sources

# Basic Comprehension

Perhaps you've heard the old saying, "You can't see the forest for the trees." To do well on a language arts test, you need to be able to see both the forest *and* the trees. In other words, you need to be able to understand both the main idea *and* the important details in a selection.

In this unit, you will learn to answer questions about main ideas and the details that support them. You will practice figuring out the meanings of unfamiliar words based on the other words around them. And, finally, you will practice applying these skills and others in reading visual information, such as graphs and tables.

# Lesson 1: Main Idea and Theme

Many of the selections on the New York Language Arts Test will be followed by a main idea question. To answer this type of question, you'll need to be able to describe what each selection is *mostly* about—in one sentence.

## Getting the Point

Doing this is easier than it sounds. In fact, you do this sort of quick summing-up all the time. Imagine that you are telling a friend about *Planet of the Apes,* an old movie you just saw on TV. You say, "It's about an astronaut who travels hundreds of years in suspended animation, then lands on a planet ruled by apes, only to learn that he is actually back on Earth."

You probably won't spend two hours describing everything that happens in the movie. You may want to mention some of the cooler things that happen, to show your friend what you mean by "suspended animation" or "ruled by apes." But those facts just support the main idea you have already described.

**Directions:** Read the selection below. It will be used to explain the tips that follow.

from
## *Forecasting the Future*
by Winnie Lujack

What will be the most important issue facing the human race in the 21st century? War and peace? Economic growth? Those are good guesses, but it's possible that the most important issue of all might be something many of us take for granted: water. A growing population and increasing levels of pollutants have made drinkable water more scarce than at any other time in human history. Although 70% of our planet is covered by water, most of it is salt water. Only about 3% of the water on Earth is fresh. Since fresh water is essential to life, having enough of it is a major concern for every person and country in the world.

Right now, about 40% of the world's population suffers water shortages, mostly in the Middle East, the Sahara Desert area of Africa, and central Asia. The western United States is also short of water. Although 60% of the land area of the United States is in the West, that area gets only 25% of the rain and snow that falls on the entire country. In California, 80% of the demand for water comes from the southern two-thirds of the state, but 70% of the state's rain falls in the north. The fastest-growing major city in the United States is Las Vegas, Nevada—located in the middle of a desert. Las Vegas faces limits on growth if its water problems cannot be solved.

Several nations in the Middle East have responded to water shortages by converting ocean water to fresh water through a process called *desalinization*. Desalinization is an expensive process, but a useful one in areas with no other water source but the oceans. Most of the fresh water used in the Persian Gulf region is desalinized. Some countries in the region also depend on lakes, rivers, and underground water supplies called *aquifers*, which in turn depend on unpredictable annual rainfall to replenish them.

In North America, the problem is not so much an overall water shortage. The real problem is that there's a lot of water in some places and not enough in others. For example, Canada has a vast supply of fresh water in the lakes and rivers of its far northern regions; large areas of Mexico and the southwestern United States, on the other hand, have severely limited water resources. A plan to pipe water across the continent was drawn up, but it was abandoned on the basis of the environmental damage that would have been caused by the construction.

The future depends on our ability to solve the problem of water shortages. We should keep in mind the words of geographer George Demko, who said, "Water is life, wealth, and power. It is far more rare, vulnerable, and precious than oil."

## Read the entire selection.

As you read a selection for the first time, ask yourself what the topic is. It is important that you read the entire selection before answering this question. Don't assume the title will tell you. The selection may be an excerpt from a larger work or be given a mysterious title to attract the reader's attention. Similarly, the author may catch the reader's attention with one topic in the introductory paragraph, then move on or narrow the focus to the real subject in the paragraphs that follow.

1. This selection is **mainly** about —
   A. global warming
   B. the increasing scarcity of water
   C. important issues in the 21st century
   D. the distribution of water around the globe

If you had read only the first couple of sentences of the selection, you might have marked choices A or C. Of course, the author quickly narrows her focus to water scarcity (B) as the issue she will address. Choice D is touched on in the selection, but it is not the main topic or issue.

## Ask yourself what point the author is trying to make about the topic.

Authors almost always have a point, or main idea, to their writing. When you think you've discovered the main idea, check to see whether it's mentioned in nearly every paragraph in at least some small way.

2. The **main** idea of the selection is that —
   A. pollution has led to water shortages in the United States and Canada
   B. desalinization is an expensive process that is widely used in the Middle East
   C. right now, about 60% of the world's population suffers water shortages
   D. water shortages are a growing concern around the world

 **Don't count on seeing the main idea stated in the selection.**

The main idea is always stated in the selection, isn't it?

Not necessarily. Writers can do whatever they please. They can come out and tell you exactly what they're talking about, or they can give you a whole bunch of hints and let you figure it out yourself. Although short essays and paragraphs often have a stated main idea, many longer works do not. Your job is to sort through all the details and ideas and put them together in a single, global statement.

Of course, there are many ways to say the same thing. Here's another main idea question about the selection you just read.

3. The **main** idea of the selection is that —
   A. some countries convert ocean water to fresh water through desalinization
   B. drinkable water is more scarce now than at any other time in human history
   C. solving the problem of water shortages may be the most important challenge of the 21st century
   D. construction on a water pipeline from Canada to the United States was abandoned

 **"Okay" answers aren't the same thing as "best" answers.**

One of the wrong answers to a main idea question may seem okay when you first read it. Don't just mark it and move on without reading the other choices first. Another choice may be better than the "okay" answer, but you'll never find it if you don't read them all.

In question number 3, choice B is "okay." It gets very close to the heart of the selection. If you read carefully, however, you will see that choice B *supports* the main idea more than it *states* the main idea.

**"Best summary" questions are just another form of main idea questions.**

Sometimes you'll be asked to choose the best summary of a selection. You should look for an answer choice that covers all major ideas in the selection. Be careful, though. Some of the choices will include information that is unimportant, factually incorrect, or not mentioned in the selection. Avoid those choices.

4. Which sentence would be the **best** summary of this selection?
   A. Many attempts to deal with worldwide water shortages have been criticized for their high costs.
   B. Seventy percent of the earth is covered by drinkable water.
   C. Increasing water shortages have led to new ideas for making more water available to areas that need it.
   D. Some cities face limits on their population growth.

Now, try two more main idea questions.

5. If you told a friend about this selection, what would be **most** important?
   A. The fastest-growing major city in the United States is Las Vegas.
   B. Although 70% of our planet is covered by water, most of it is salt water.
   C. Aquifers depend on unpredictable annual rainfall to replenish them.
   D. Having enough water is a concern for every person and country in the world.

6. Which title would be the **best** summary for this selection?
   A. "Water Conservation Tips"
   B. "Where Will Our Water Come From?"
   C. "Population Growth: When Will It End?"
   D. "Desalinization: An Expensive Solution"

**Use your sense of a story's meaning to answer questions about theme.**

Some "main idea" questions will focus on the theme of a story, rather than the main idea of a nonfiction selection. Use your sense of the story's meaning to determine its theme. On the following page is a folktale that will help you practice identifying the "main idea" in fiction. Read the selection and answer the questions, then check your answers in the back of the book.

## Summing Up

As you answer main idea questions, keep the following tips in mind:
- First, read the entire selection, then identify its topic.
- Look for the author's point among the answer choices.
- Do not expect to see a stated main idea, but be prepared just in case it shows up.
- Don't be misled by answers that seem "okay" but aren't quite right.
- Understand that finding a "best summary" is similar to finding the "main idea."
- Use your sense of a story's meaning to answer questions about theme.

# PRACTICE SELECTION

**Directions:** Read the selection and answer the questions that follow.

## The Panther and the Heron

a Hmong fable retold by J. M. Wasson

In a steamy jungle in Asia, a sleek black panther prowled through the thick undergrowth searching for his evening meal. His dark fur hid him from his prey as he padded softly on the jungle floor. He was a mighty hunter, feared by the other animals for his sharp teeth and long dangerous claws.

> The Hmong people are from Laos, a country in southeast Asia.

Later that evening, as Panther was gulping down his supper, a splinter of bone became stuck between his teeth. Try as he might, he could not remove it. His mouth was on fire, and he howled in pain throughout the night. He couldn't eat and he couldn't sleep.

At daybreak, Panther saw Heron standing in the shallow water at the river's edge. Heron had just caught a large fish and was about to eat it for his breakfast when Panther called to him.

"Help me, brother Heron, for I am in great pain. Your long beak can quickly remove the cause of my agony."

Heron, being a good-natured soul, took pity on Panther. He dropped the squirming fish back into the muddy water and flew over to Panther's side.

The big cat carefully opened his swollen jaw to let Heron remove the offending splinter. Heron could see that Panther's jaw was painfully sore. But even so, the sight of those long, sharp teeth gave him a start. The kindhearted bird quickly pecked the bone from between Panther's teeth. Panther cried out in relief and gratitude.

Finally free from pain, a grateful Panther promised always to be kind to Heron in the future. "Thank you, brother Heron. In times of drought when there are few fish to be found," he said, "I will share my food with you to repay your good deed."

But it wasn't long at all until Panther forgot what Heron had done for him. Selfish thoughts rose up in his head, pushing his promise aside. "Why should I share with that twig of a bird?" he asked. "He's so skinny; he doesn't need to eat much. Not like me. I'm large, powerful, and muscular. I need all the food I can get to keep in this fine form." He admired his reflection in a still pool of water before taking a long, satisfying drink. Then and there, he resolved never to give any food to Heron.

Drought came to the jungle. The rains stopped and the river began to dry up. Fish were hard to find and Heron grew hungry. His empty stomach reminded him of Panther's promise. He went to Panther and said, "Do you remember the good deed I did for you by pecking the bone from between your teeth?"

Panther snarled at him and turned his head away.

But Heron continued. "You promised me in times of drought that you would share your meal with me. I am hungry, Panther. Please give me some food to eat today."

There was no persuading Panther to honor his bargain. He growled loudly, "Go away, you miserable bird! What good are you to me now that my pain is gone?"

Heron was furious. He cried, "Panther, you are not grateful for what I did. All you care about is yourself!"

Panther said, "Foolish little twig, don't you know that I eat other animals? I did you a favor by not eating you when your head was in my mouth." Then he snapped his jaws at Heron, flashing his long white teeth in warning.

Shocked and frightened, Heron did not know what to say or do. This jungle was no longer a good place to live, he decided. So he flew south along the river to a new home far, far away.

Several days later, Panther was eating his dinner when he let out a cry. Once again, a piece of bone had become stuck between his teeth. The pain was unbearable. Frantic, Panther looked around for Heron. "Where are you, my feathery friend? Come help me remove this terrible bone and I will reward you handsomely," he cried.

But Heron was nowhere to be found, and Panther was left alone with his troubles.

# Sample Main Idea Questions

**Directions:** Read each question and circle the letter of the correct answer.

1. This selection is **mainly** about —
   A. courage
   B. jealousy
   C. selfishness
   D. physical pain

2. Which of the following tells the theme of the story?
   A. The early bird gets the worm.
   B. Birds of a feather flock together.
   C. Always try to turn the other cheek.
   D. Don't bite the hand that feeds you.

3. Which of the following is the **best** summary of this selection?
   A. A panther breaks his promise to a heron who helps him.
   B. A panther promises to share his food with a heron.
   C. A heron helps a panther by picking a splinter out of his teeth.
   D. A heron refuses to help a panther who has a splinter in his teeth.

4. Read the following paragraph from the selection, then answer the question below.

   Panther said, "Foolish little twig, don't you know that I eat other animals? I did you a favor by not eating you when your head was in my mouth." Then he snapped his jaws at Heron, flashing his long white teeth in warning.

   The **main** idea of this paragraph is that Panther —
   A. has long teeth
   B. is always hungry
   C. behaves like a bully
   D. did the heron a favor

# Additional Practice Questions

**Directions:** Now answer some other types of questions about the reading selection. You can learn about these question types in other lessons of this book.

5. What caused Panther's pain?
   A. A trap
   B. A bone
   C. A bullet
   D. A piece of wood

6. Which of these occurred **first**?
   A. Heron helps Panther.
   B. Panther threatens Heron.
   C. A drought makes Heron hungry.
   D. Panther makes a promise to Heron.

7. The author's purpose in this selection is to —
   A. describe the animals found in Laos
   B. inform the reader about Hmong culture
   C. persuade the reader to dislike Panther
   D. teach the reader through the use of a story

8. From reading this selection, you can tell that —
   A. Heron is a foolish character
   B. Heron learns from experience
   C. Heron will never go hungry again
   D. Heron always lacked trust in Panther

9. Which word **best** describes Panther?
   A. Odd
   B. Clumsy
   C. Careless
   D. Stingy

10. This selection would **most likely** be found in a book with the title —
    A. *Folktales and Fables from Asia*
    B. *Animals from Around the World*
    C. *Drought and its Effects on the Food Chain*
    D. *Things I Learned in Preschool*

# Lesson 2: Details and Sequencing of Events

Two plus two is four. The capital of New York is Albany. Andrew Jackson was president from 1829 to 1837. The chemical formula for water is $H_2O$. These are all facts. Facts are the raw materials of knowledge. Broader topics such as the struggle for equal rights, the origins of the English language, or the manufacture of soft drinks are based on facts like the ones listed above.

Most stories and articles are filled with facts. These facts (called **details** in reading selections) are important to writing because they support the author's main idea.

On the New York English Language Arts Test, you will be asked questions about details in reading selections. Some detail questions will ask you for a single fact from the selection. Others will expect you to understand how the details relate to the main idea of the selection. Some may ask you to recall in what order the events described in a selection took place.

 **The answers to detail questions are always given in the selection.**

The answers to questions about details will be given to you in the selection. All you need to do is find them.

**Directions:** Read the selection below. It will be used to explain the tips that follow.

## A Homecoming for Horses
### by Leslie Roach

The horse has a unique place in the history of the American West. Horses are believed to have originated in North America, but after 11,000 B.C., they seem to have died out on this continent, along with a number of other beasts, such as the sloth and woolly mammoth. Horses fared better on the Asian and European continents, and when the Spanish came to the "New World," they reintroduced the majestic *Equus caballus* to its native habitat. It quickly became one of the hardiest creatures of the frontier, changing the Indians' lives and shaping the destiny of our nation.

Fossil remains of ancient horses have been found all over the globe, except on the continent of Australia. Archaeologists believe that since the oldest remains occur on the North American continent, the horse originated here and migrated from Alaska to Siberia across the Beringia land bridge, which was exposed thousands of years ago.

*Eohippus* roamed North America 55 million years ago. It was small, only 10 to 20 inches tall, and it had several toes on each foot. Ten million years later came *Orohippis*. Another ten million years, and the species earned a new name, *Mesohippus*, and was by then a creature that looked vaguely like the modern horse. Others to follow were the *Miohippis* and the *Parahippis*. The *Meryhippus*, about 19 million years ago, had teeth suitable for eating grass. The true horse, *Equus*, came along one and a half million years ago, eventually becoming today's *Equus caballus*.

But Native Americans had never set eyes on *Equus* until the Spanish conquistadors arrived in the 16th century. Horses enabled the Spanish conquerors to subdue the Central American Aztec nation. The first "cowboys" were born in the next century, when the Spanish landlords trained their Indian slaves to tend their expanding herds. Those horses that escaped and became wild thrived on the grasslands of the western American plains. These *mestengos*, as the Spanish called them, were smaller and scruffier than their forebears, but swift and hardy, requiring very little water.

Wild mustangs formed the backbone of the Indian resistance in the west. On horseback, the Apaches were able to drive their enemies away. The Utes, Dakotas, Cheyennes, Crows, and Kiowas also learned to ride horses, using them in their buffalo hunts. But it was the proud and fierce Comanches who raised riding to an art form. They virtually lived on horseback, becoming "one with the horse." Every Comanche man, woman, and child could ride. They copied Spanish bits and bridles and made saddles of buffalo hide. But their great invention was a buffalo-hide thong that let the brave drop down to the side of the horse, where he would be protected from arrows and bullets. The Comanches were famous for being able to shoot arrows at full gallop with deadly accuracy.

European settlers eventually overcame the Indians, but the horse has remained a vital part of the Great Plains tradition. Although many of today's ranchers use their pickup trucks more than their mounts, the old-time cowboys of the Chisholm Trail depended on horses to move their cattle from Texas through Oklahoma to Kansas and back.

**TIP #2    Use the selection to check your memory of details.**

Perhaps you get a detail question that you think you can answer from memory. If you remember the detail, you can probably remember where it is found in the selection. Go back to the selection and double-check yourself before marking the answer.

1. Which nation virtually lived on horseback?
   A. Utes
   B. Aztecs
   C. Apaches
   D. Comanches

## Skim the selection to find a key word or phrase from the question.

If you didn't pick up the answer to a detail question while you were reading, you will have to go back and find it in the selection. This step doesn't really involve normal reading. Instead, you simply go looking for words related to the detail.

For example, you might be asked the following question about the selection:

2. When did the Spanish conquistadors bring horses to the American continent?
   A. 11,000 B.C.
   B. 15th century A.D.
   C. 16th century A.D.
   D. 17th century A.D.

**Skimming** is a way of running your eyes over the selection while looking for a specific word or phrase. When you're skimming, don't stop until you find what you're looking for. In this case, you could skim the selection to look for the words "Spanish conquistador." The correct answer to this question is found in paragraph 4.

## Connect details to the main idea to determine which details are important.

The most important details are those that support the main idea. The main idea of this selection is that "the horse has a unique place in the history of the American west." The selection supports this idea by discussing the "homecoming" story of horses' extinction in North America and their reintroduction. It goes on to discuss ways in which horses have shaped the history of our country. Given this information, answer the following question:

3. When summarizing this selection, which of these facts would be **most** important to include?
   A. After 11,000 B.C., horses seem to have died out on this continent.
   B. On horseback, the Apaches were able to drive out their enemies.
   C. *Eohippus* was small, only 10 to 20 inches tall, and it had several toes on each foot.
   D. Those horses that escaped and became wild thrived on the grasslands of the western American plains.

## Use an outline to organize details.

While outlining during the test may prove to be too time-consuming for you, outlining is an excellent strategy for organizing details. Converting the discussion above to outline form, we might diagram the selection this way:

Horses Have a Unique History in the American West

I. They have had a "homecoming."

    A. They originated in North America.

    B. They became extinct on this continent.

    C. They were reintroduced by the Spanish.

II. They have shaped the history of our country.

    A. They helped the Indian resistance.

    B. **?**

4. Which of the following ideas **best** completes the outline?

    A. The Comanches virtually lived on horseback.

    B. They were important to cattlemen in the West.

    C. They migrated from Alaska to Siberia across the Beringia land bridge.

    D. Native Americans had never set eyes on *Equus* until the Spanish conquistadors arrived.

**Understand the order in which the events take place.**

Writers don't have to tell events in the order in which they really happened. However, *you* may be asked to put events in order on a reading test.

When you read an order-of-events question, you don't have to worry about *every* event in the selection—just those in the question and answer choices. You may find it helpful to put those events on a time line.

5. Which of these species originated **first**?

    A. *Equus*

    B. *Eohippus*

    C. *Mesohippus*

    D. *Equus caballus*

## Summing Up

As you answer questions about details, keep in mind the following tips:

- The answers to detail questions are always given in the selection.
- Use the selection to check your memory of details.
- Skim the selection for key words from the question or answer choices.
- Important details can be connected to the main idea.
- Use an outline to organize details.
- Read carefully to understand the order of events in the selection.

**Directions:** Read the selection and answer the questions that follow.

# The Martians Have Landed!

by Arthur Figgis

Before there was television, radio was the most popular form of home entertainment in America. In those days (1920–1950), radio was much like television without the pictures. Radio stations broadcasted dramatized stories. It was up to the listeners to imagine what was happening, based on the voices and sounds that came through the speakers. In addition to this type of entertainment, radio also provided news and music. Radio was as important in its heyday as TV is to many families today.

On Sunday, October 30, 1938, millions of listeners were tuned in to one of the most popular shows on the air, NBC's *The Charlie McCarthy Show*. A much smaller number of people were listening to the low-rated *Mercury Theatre on the Air* on CBS. The Mercury Players, led by their 23-year-old star and director, Orson Welles, were presenting a version of the science-fiction story *The War of the Worlds*, which is about a Martian invasion of Earth.

This broadcast was unusual because it didn't sound like a normal radio play. It began with a few minutes of music. Then an announcer broke in to tell the audience that scientists were reporting strange activity on the planet Mars.

The music then returned and, later, so did the announcer. This time, he said that Martian spaceships had landed near Grovers Mills, a real town in the state of New Jersey. The rest of the program sounded like an actual news broadcast, which reported that New York, Chicago, San Francisco, and other large American cities were being destroyed by Martians.

At the start of *The War of the Worlds*, the announcer told the radio audience that what they were about to hear was not real but just a radio play. Many listeners apparently missed that announcement. Orson Welles's deep, authoritative voice pulled them into the fantasy. He sounded so serious, so convincing. In their imaginations, listeners magnified his words with mental images that caused terror in their hearts. They became certain that Earth really was being invaded by Martians. As word spread, more people tuned in, and a full-scale panic soon began.

Roads in New Jersey were jammed with carloads of people fleeing from the imagined invasion. In New York City, people streamed out of restaurants to hurry home. Some U.S. Navy sailors were called back to their ships to go on alert. People cried and prayed, absolutely sure that Earth was being overrun by creatures from another planet.

Meanwhile, back in the studio, the Mercury Players had no idea what kind of <u>havoc</u> their play was causing. The broadcast ended with an announcement that it had all been in fun.

After it was over, CBS, Welles, and the Mercury Players were threatened with lawsuits by people who had been injured or suffered property damage in the panic. All of the lawsuits were soon dropped, however. The *Mercury Theatre on the Air*, which had been in danger of being canceled for low ratings before *The War of the Worlds*, became a big hit. Orson Welles soon left radio and later became prominent in the movie industry as an actor and a director.

Why did the panic happen? Were people simply more <u>gullible</u> in 1938 than they are today? Certainly, they had less experience with modern electronic media than we do. There was a strong faith that if something was broadcast on the radio, it had to be true.

The panic also might have had something to do with the fact that America was a nervous place in the fall of 1938. European nations had narrowly escaped going to war in September, and Americans had anxiously followed the news on the radio. Also in September, the northeastern United States had been hit without warning by a rare hurricane. Weather forecasters missed it completely, and over 700 people died.

And if all that wasn't spooky enough, along came Orson Welles, the Mercury Players, and thousands of make-believe Martians. Welles had picked the right time of year to put a scare into the country: *The War of the Worlds* was broadcast on the night before Halloween.

# Sample Detail Questions

**Directions:** Read each question and circle the letter of the correct answer.

1. In 1938, Orson Welles was —
   A. a movie actor
   B. a movie director
   C. director and star of The Mercury Players
   D. director of NBC's *The Charlie McCarthy Show*

2. All of these are examples of what happened in reaction to *The War of the Worlds* broadcast **except** —
   A. sailors were sent back to their ships
   B. carloads of people jammed the highways
   C. several people were killed during the panic
   D. word spread that the Martians had landed

3. When summarizing why America was a nervous place in the fall of 1938, which of these details would be **most** important to include?
   A. Some European nations had narrowly avoided going to war.
   B. If people heard something on the radio, they believed it was true.
   C. Roads in New Jersey were jammed with carloads of people.
   D. Orson Welles left radio after *The War of the Worlds* was broadcast.

4. According to the selection, which of these occurred **last**?
   A. CBS was threatened with lawsuits.
   B. *The War of the Worlds* was broadcast.
   C. Orson Welles became a movie actor and director.
   D. An unexpected hurricane struck the eastern United States.

# Additional Practice Questions

**Directions:** Now answer some other types of questions about the reading selection. You can learn about these question types in other lessons of this book.

5. The author gives you enough evidence to think that the Mercury Players —
   A. presented *The Charlie McCarthy Show*
   B. became more popular after *The War of the Worlds*
   C. regularly featured music and news in their radio plays
   D. were found guilty of causing panic with *The War of the Worlds*

6. The word *havoc* is used in this selection to mean —
   A. worry
   B. disorder
   C. celebration
   D. entertainment

7. The broadcast of *The War of the Worlds* was a good thing for Orson Welles because it —
   A. started Welles's long and successful radio career
   B. gained listeners for the *Mercury Theatre on the Air*
   C. made science fiction more popular than ever before
   D. caused the cancellation of *The Charlie McCarthy Show*

8. In this selection, the word *gullible* means —
   A. easily fooled
   B. highly critical
   C. quick to judge
   D. somewhat understanding

9. This selection is **mainly** about —
   A. the brilliant young actor, Orson Welles
   B. a Martian landing at Grovers Mills, New Jersey
   C. the importance of radio broadcasts in the 1930s
   D. a radio show that convinced people of a Martian attack

10. Which of the following experiences would help you most in understanding this selection?
   A. Viewing close-up videos of the surface of Mars
   B. Turning on a radio news show while in a traffic jam
   C. Looking at a picture book of Orson Welles's performances
   D. Listening to recordings of *Mercury Theatre* radio dramas

# Lesson 3: Vocabulary in Context

Numismatist? Indefatigable? Quisling? Traduce? Zyzzyva?

*Oh, no! Do I have to know every word in the English language to pass the test?*

Of course not. No one does. You see, the test writers don't expect you to have a <u>phenomenal</u> (extraordinary) vocabulary. They *do* expect you to have some skills that will help you figure out new words.

You won't be given <u>isolated</u> (set apart from the others) words and asked to provide definitions for them. What you will get is an occasional vocabulary word within a reading selection. This means you'll have plenty of information—right in the selection—to help you determine what the word means.

So don't think you have to memorize the whole dictionary. All you need to learn between now and test day is how to figure out what a word means by the way it is used in a sentence and by the words that surround it in a selection.

In general, you can expect that the selection will provide enough information to help you figure out the meaning of any vocabulary word. This lesson will give you tips to help you identify that information and show you how to answer a variety of vocabulary questions.

---

In case you want to amaze your friends with your vocabulary knowledge, here are the definitions of the words listed at the beginning of this lesson. Feel free to slip them into conversations whenever you like:

- **numismatist** (new-MIZ-ma-tist): a person who studies and collects coins. *My uncle, the numismatist, has a 1903 penny.*
- **indefatigable** (in-da-FAT-ig-uh-bul): incapable of getting tired. *He never stops studying. He's indefatigable!*
- **quisling** (QUIZ-ling): traitor. *Don't wear that South High sweatshirt here at North High. What are you, some kind of quisling?*
- **traduce** (truh-DOOSE; rhymes with "loose"): to speak falsely about. *You have traduced cafeteria food. It's actually very good.*
- **zyzzyva** (ZIZ-uh-vuh): the last word in many dictionaries: a type of plant-eating insect found in tropical regions of North and South America. *Hand me the newspaper so I can swat that zyzzyva, will you?*

---

**Directions:** Read the selection below. It will be used to explain the tips that follow.

from
# *Life on the Mississippi*
by Mark Twain

Now when I had mastered the language of this water and had come to know every <u>trifling</u> feature that bordered the great river as familiarly as I knew the letters of the alphabet, I had made a valuable acquisition. But I had lost something, too. I had lost something which could never be restored to me while I lived. All the grace, the beauty, the poetry had gone out of the <u>majestic</u>

> **Mark Twain** is the pseudonym, or "pen name," of Samuel Clemens (1835–1910), who grew up in Hannibal, Missouri on the Mississippi River. His most famous characters are Tom Sawyer and Huckleberry Finn.

river! I still keep in mind a certain wonderful sunset which I witnessed when steamboating was new to me. A broad expanse of the river was turned to blood; in the middle distance the red <u>hue</u> brightened into gold, through which a solitary log came floating, black and <u>conspicuous</u>; in one place a long slanting mark lay sparkling upon the water; in another the surface was broken by boiling, tumbling rings, that were as many-tinted as an opal; where the ruddy flush was faintest, was a smooth spot that was covered with graceful circles and radiating lines, ever so delicately traced; the shore on our left was densely wooded, and the <u>somber</u> shadow that fell from this forest was broken in one place by a long ruffled trail that shone like silver; and high above the forest wall a clean-stemmed dead tree waved a single leafy bough that glowed like a flame in the unobstructed <u>splendor</u> that was flowing from the sun. There were graceful curves, reflected images, woody heights, soft distances: and over the whole scene, far and near, the dissolving lights drifted steadily, enriching it, every passing moment, with new marvels of coloring.

I stood like one bewitched. I drank it in, in a speechless rapture. The world was new to me, and I had never seen anything like this at home. But as I have said, a day came when I began to cease from noting the glories and the charms which the moon and the sun and the twilight <u>wrought</u> upon the river's face; another day came when I ceased altogether to note them. Then, if that sunset scene had been repeated, I should have looked upon it without rapture, and should have commented upon it, inwardly, after this <u>fashion</u>: This sun means that we are going to have wind tomorrow; that floating log means that the river is rising, small thanks to it; that slanting mark on the water refers to a bluff reef which is going to kill somebody's steamboat one of these nights. . . .

**Look in the selection for other words with a similar meaning.**

Look nearby for words that have the same—or almost the same—meaning as the vocabulary word. Read the following sentence and answer number 1.

> All the grace, the beauty, the poetry had gone out of the <u>majestic</u> river!

1. Underline words in the sentence that have a similar meaning to the word *majestic*.

2. In this sentence, the word *majestic* means —
   A. stormy
   B. energetic
   C. grand
   D. powerful

If something is graceful, beautiful, and poetic, it isn't likely to be *stormy, energetic,* or *powerful*. It might, however, be *grand*.

 **Try to fit the new word into a category.**

Sometimes a vocabulary word will fit into a group of other, similar things. Once you determine in what group the word fits, you'll be better able to figure out its meaning. This technique often works well with words that have specialized or technical meanings.

Read the following excerpt from the selection and answer number 3.

> A broad expanse of the river was turned to blood; in the middle distance the red <u>hue</u> brightened into gold. . . .

3. What is the meaning of *hue* in this selection?
   A. Color
   B. Sky
   C. Sun
   D. Blood

*Hue* appears in the sentence along with *red* and *gold*. Red and gold are colors, so you can guess that *hue* means *color*. *Hue* is a specialized word that applies to art.

 **Look for opposites.**

If you can use information in a sentence to figure out what a word's opposite meaning is, you can make a good guess about the meaning of the word itself. Look at the excerpt below:

[T]he <u>somber</u> shadow that fell from this forest was broken in one place
by a long ruffled trail that shone like silver. . . .

4. The word *somber* in this selection means —
   A. ugly
   B. dark
   C. bright
   D. frightening

The selection tells us, "the somber shadow . . . was broken in one place by a . . .
trail that shone like silver." This sets up an opposite in our mind's eye. A *somber* trail
broken by a shining place. Since the shining place is bright, the *somber* trail must be
the opposite—*dark*.

**Think of words that are "cousins" of the unknown word.**

Read the question below.

5. In this selection, *splendor* means —
   A. fierceness
   B. colorfulness
   C. enormous size
   D. great brightness

Maybe you've never seen *splendor* before, but you probably know its first cousin,
*splendid.* People may say that someone did a "splendid job." You think of *splendid*
as "excellent." Excellent is not fierce or colorful or huge. But is it "bright" or "greatly
bright"? If all else fails, it's a good guess.

Also, look at the sentence in which the word appears. The phrases "glowed like
a flame" and "flowing from the sun" also are clues to the correct answer.

**Plug in the answer choices.**

By the time you've tried these tips, you've probably made a good guess. But you may
not know for sure until you try it out. Once you've got the answer choices narrowed
down, plug in each one to see if it makes sense in the sentence.

The best answer choice may not have exactly the same meaning as the unknown
word. Also, the substitute word may take an "a" instead of an "an," or have some
other problem that shows up when you try to plug it in this way. But the one that
makes the *most* sense in the sentence is the correct answer.

Try this technique on the sentence and question below.

> . . . I had mastered the language of this water and had come to know every <u>trifling</u> feature that bordered the great river as familiarly as I knew the letters of the alphabet. . . .

6. In this sentence, *trifling* means —
   A. famous
   B inspiring
   C. dangerous
   D. unimportant

Twain is describing how well he knows every feature of the river. He compares the way he knows these *trifling* features to the way he knows the "letters of the alphabet." Here's how the answer choices work when plugged into the sentence:

> I had mastered the language of this water and had come to know every famous feature that bordered the great river as familiarly as I knew the letters of the alphabet. . . .

> I had mastered the language of this water and had come to know every inspiring feature that bordered the great river as familiarly as I knew the letters of the alphabet. . . .

> I had mastered the language of this water and had come to know every dangerous feature that bordered the great river as familiarly as I knew the letters of the alphabet. . . .

> I had mastered the language of this water and had come to know every unimportant feature that bordered the great river as familiarly as I knew the letters of the alphabet. . . .

Neither the river's features nor the alphabet's letters seem very *famous, inspiring,* or *dangerous.* But they do seem *unimportant* when considered alone. Like the letters of the alphabet, which are virtually meaningless until they are put together to form a word, each "trifling" feature of the river is insignificant until it is considered as a part of the river as a whole.

## Watch out for words with more than one meaning.

Multiple-meaning words are words such as *plot,* which can mean "a small piece of ground," "a secret plan," or "the sequence of events in a story."

Read the excerpt below, then answer number 7.

Then, if that sunset scene had been repeated, I should have . . . commented upon it, inwardly, after this <u>fashion</u>. . . .

7. In this selection, *fashion* means —
   A. dress
   B. creation
   C. manner
   D. clothing style

*Dress* (A) and *clothing style* (D) are pretty easy to rule out. Choice B is a bit trickier. One meaning of *fashion* is "to create," as in "to fashion a metal bracelet"; but that meaning doesn't make sense in this context. The only meaning that works is *manner* (C). If you're still uncertain, plug it in to make sure.

## Summing Up

As you answer vocabulary questions, keep in mind the following tips:
- Look for other words with a similar meaning.
- Try to fit the new word into a category.
- Look for opposites.
- Think of words that are "cousins" of the unknown word.
- Plug in the answer choices.
- Watch out for words with more than one meaning.

## PRACTICE SELECTION

**Directions:** Read the selection and answer the questions that follow.

# *Rachel Carson*

by Greta Anderson

In 1958, Rachel Carson began planning her next book—a book that was to have an enormous impact on the nation and on the world. She had already written two best-selling books, both about the ocean. Carson had fallen in love with the ocean as a child, long before she'd even seen it, mostly through reading poems that described the ocean's power and beauty.

In college, she studied biology, then worked for the U.S. Fish and Wildlife Service. She had always wanted to be a writer, and knew that by becoming a biologist she had given herself something to write about.

This new book did not promise to be a fun book to write, however. Her earlier books celebrated all the life forms she'd come to know. But life, as she knew it, was changing. Fishes were getting sick and dying, and lately she hadn't seen as many butterflies as she was accustomed to seeing. She had a <u>hunch</u> why this was, and she hoped her scientific training could help her <u>verify</u> that hunch.

In 1958, and for a whole decade after, giant trucks would rumble through the towns and suburbs of America, puffing out clouds of a chemical, DDT, that killed mosquitoes and other "bad" insects. Low-flying planes would cruise over farmland, blanketing it with DDT. No one likes mosquitoes or the insects that damage crops; mosquitoes aren't just bothersome, they carry diseases like typhus and malaria. But something told Carson that this approach wasn't the best.

So many important questions had not been answered. Does this chemical kill "good" insects, too? Does it harm the birds and fish that eat all kinds of insects? Nobody seemed to be asking these questions. People were told to be glad that science had found a way to get rid of the pests.

Meanwhile, Carson received a letter from a friend who had read her books on the ocean and was an <u>avid</u> bird-watcher. What Carson suspected, this woman knew from years of intensive observation: The bird population had diminished drastically. Nature was sick, and it was because of those low-flying planes that came around all too often. She'd written a letter to the editor of her paper, but that wasn't enough. Could Carson help?

Once Rachel Carson got started, she heard from scientists who were studying this problem in depth. No one was listening to what they had to say, either. After several tough years of work, Carson's book, *Silent Spring*, took shape. When it was published, it was instantly popular among the millions of Americans who had begun to distrust the DDT clouds that made them instinctively run for cover. The people demanded to know whether DDT was necessary. The president at the time, John F. Kennedy, wanted to know, too.

Chemical companies, believing in their product, tried to discredit Carson's book. Still, her original hunch that DDT does more harm than good quickly gained enough scientific backing to make it a fact. Within several years, the pesticide was banned in the United States, as well as in many foreign countries.

*Silent Spring* explained the science in a way people could understand. It was also beautifully written. The book opens up like a fairy tale:

> There was once a town in the heart of America where all life seemed to live in harmony with its surroundings. The town lay in the midst of a checkerboard of prosperous farms, with fields of grain and hillsides of orchards. . . .

But the narrative soon becomes <u>ominous</u>:

> Then a strange blight crept over the area. . . . There was a strange stillness.

Spring arrived, Carson explains, but not with the usual cheerful sounds of birds and bees.

Carson died of cancer just two years after the book came out in 1964. Her work has saved countless lives by opening people's eyes to the dangers of DDT. Other pesticides have now replaced DDT, and the government regulates their use. As part of Rachel Carson's <u>legacy</u>, people have become more cautious about the chemicals they use.

# Sample Vocabulary Questions

**Directions:** Read each question and circle the letter of the correct answer.

1. In this selection, the word *verify* means —
   A. try
   B. prove
   C. investigate
   D. understand

2. What does the word *avid* mean in this selection?
   A. Casual
   B. Restless
   C. Beginning
   D. Dedicated

3. In paragraph 4, the word *bad* is in quotation marks because —
   A. mosquitoes are actually beneficial insects
   B. "good" animals, such as birds, were also harmed
   C. labeling insects as good or bad is overly simplistic
   D. only the author thinks the insects that were killed are bad

4. The word *hunch* in this selection means —
   A. an educated guess
   B. an obsessive worry
   C. a physical deformity
   D. a mistaken piece of information

5. The word *ominous* is used in this selection to mean —
   A. cold
   B. scary
   C. violent
   D. peaceful

6. In the **last** sentence of the selection, the word *legacy* means —
   A. book
   B. wishes
   C. testimony
   D. contribution

# Additional Practice Questions

**Directions:** Now answer some other types of questions about the reading selection. You can learn about these question types in other lessons of this book.

7. What is Rachel Carson's book, *Silent Spring*, **mainly** about?
   A. Birds and bird-watching
   B. The ocean's power and beauty
   C. How to reduce pollution in the cities
   D. The effects of DDT on the environment

8. Which of these happened **first**?
   A. Carson decided to write a book about DDT.
   B. Carson noticed that some species were not healthy.
   C. Carson heard from a friend who was a bird-watcher.
   D. Carson's friend wrote a letter to the editor of her paper.

9. The selection gives you reason to believe that —
   A. *Silent Spring* was Carson's most important book
   B. the makers of DDT did not read the book *Silent Spring*
   C. President Kennedy's interest in *Silent Spring* made it popular
   D. Carson's books about the ocean were more difficult for her to write

10. Which of these expresses the author's point of view toward Carson's work?
    A. Critical
    B. Neutral
    C. Appreciative
    D. Condescending

# Lesson 4: Visual Information Sources

You might not believe this, but the people who wrote this book are mind readers. We know that right now, after three lessons of this book, some of the students in your very own classroom—maybe even you—are thinking, "This stuff is fine for school and the state test, but what does it have to do with real life?"

The answer is: plenty. Just in case you don't believe us, however, Lesson 4 is packed with real-life stuff: diagrams that show how things work, advertisements for things you can buy, directions for doing things, and lots of other stuff you might read during an average day.

## Different Kinds of Information

Written information doesn't come only in sentences and paragraphs. It also can be organized and presented in other ways, such as in tables, graphs, time lines, diagrams, and advertisements.

**Know how to identify and read a table.**

Tables are used to display information in a way that is easy to read. A table has five distinguishing characteristics:

- cells—the boxes in which information is given
- rows—horizontal groupings to which cells belong
- columns—vertical groupings to which cells belong
- labels—separate boxes that explain what the cells represent
- titles—labels that explain what is shown in entire tables

The following table shows the heart rates for six students riding a roller coaster at an amusement park. The **rows** (left-to-right) and **columns** (up-and-down) have **labels** that show what information is contained in them. Each box containing information is called a **cell**.

**Heart Rates (in beats per minute) of Six Students
at Various Points During a Roller Coaster Ride**

| Student | At rest away from amusement park | Waiting in line for roller coaster | In roller coaster at start of ride | In roller coaster at beginning of first drop |
|---|---|---|---|---|
| #1 | 78 | 83 | 93 | 176 |
| #2 | 74 | 78 | 88 | 158 |
| #3 | 85 | 84 | 90 | 189 |
| #4 | 82 | 83 | 93 | 168 |
| #5 | 75 | 78 | 89 | 192 |
| #6 | 80 | 85 | 95 | 201 |

label

row

cell

column

What a table tells you depends on which direction you read it. When you read the numbers in this table from left to right in any row, you see one student's heart rate data under different circumstances. When you read the numbers from top to bottom in any column, you can compare different students' heart rates under the same circumstance.

The number in each cell reflects the relationship between the row and the column to which the cell belongs. For example, the cell at Row 2, Column 2 shows that while waiting in line for the roller coaster (the label of Column 2 tells you this), Student #2 (the label of Row 2 tells you this) has a heart rate of 78 beats per minute.

## PRACTICE ACTIVITY

**Directions:** Use the heart-rate table above to answer questions 1–3.

1. Which student had the highest heart rate while waiting for the roller coaster?

   _____

2. Which student had a heart rate of 89 at the start of the ride?

   _____

3. The table provides evidence that, in general, the students' heart rates —
   A. did not change while they waited in line
   B. were highest at the roller coaster's first drop
   C. were lower while waiting in line than at rest
   D. increased more at the first drop than the last drop

## Learn about the different kinds of graphs and their purposes.

Like tables, graphs also put information into a form that is easy to see. There are different kinds of graphs for different purposes. This section will review circle graphs, bar graphs, and line graphs.

**Fish Caught in Blue Lake During August**

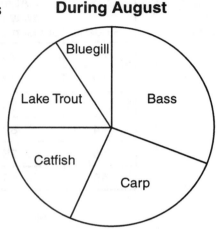

## Circle graphs

A circle graph, or pie chart, shows the parts of a whole and how different parts of a group compare to each other. Circle graphs are divided into sections, or "slices." These sections represent percentages, with the entire pie representing the whole, or 100%. You can see this in the circle graph to the right.

## PRACTICE ACTIVITY

**Directions:** Use the circle graph above to answer questions 4 and 5.

4. About what percentage of the Blue Lake catch was carp?

_____

5. In August, what two types of fish together made up more than half of the total catch?

_____

## Bar graphs

While circle graphs give you the percentage or portion of the whole, bar graphs give you the actual numbers. They use **horizontal** (left-to-right) and **vertical** (up-and-down) axes to display a relationship between groups of similar things.

You could use a bar graph to compare the number of different varieties of fish caught in Blue Lake.

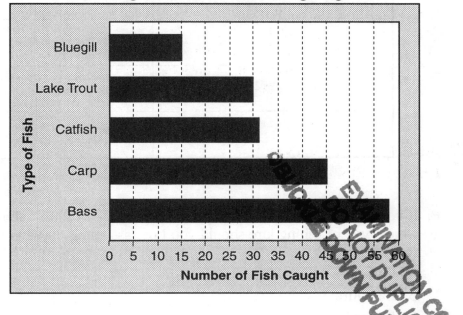

**Fish Caught in Blue Lake During August**

In this bar graph, the kinds of fish are shown on the vertical axis. The number of these kinds of fish caught in Blue Lake is shown on the horizontal axis.

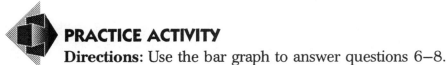

## PRACTICE ACTIVITY

**Directions:** Use the bar graph to answer questions 6–8.

6. How many carp were caught in August?

_____

7. In the space below, put the information from the bar graph into table form. Be sure to title the table and label the rows and columns clearly and correctly. Refer to the table section of this lesson if you need help.

|  |  |
|--|--|
|  |  |
|  |  |
|  |  |
|  |  |

8. If you wanted to catch as many fish as possible in Blue Lake during August, which type of fishing lure should you buy (assuming that there are no 'crossover' types of lures)?
   A. Carp lure
   B. Bass lure
   C. Bluegill lure
   D. Catfish lure

## Line graphs

Line graphs are meant primarily to show how the **variable** on the horizontal axis changes when it is affected by a variable on the vertical axis. For each unit on the horizontal line (*months* in the graph below), a point corresponds to a number on the vertical line *(gallons sold)*.

Line graphs show **relationships** between the variables. Each point is connected to the ones around it so that any **pattern**, or **trend**, can be easily viewed.

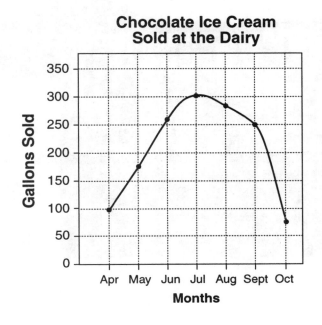

**PRACTICE ACTIVITY**

**Directions:** Use the line graph to answer questions 9 and 10.

9. What was the **least** number of gallons sold during the period shown?

_____

10. According to the graph, which statement is correct?
    A. Chocolate ice cream sales peaked in August, then fell steadily.
    B. In May, the dairy sold 200 gallons of chocolate ice cream.
    C. Chocolate ice cream sales dropped sharply from September to October.
    D. The same number of gallons was sold in May and September.

**Identify persuasive techniques in advertisements.**

An advertisement is a visual information source that tells about a product or service. Ads use facts, opinions, and other claims to try to persuade you to buy the product or use the service. Many ads use photos, drawings, or other graphics in addition to written words.

Look at the following advertisement.

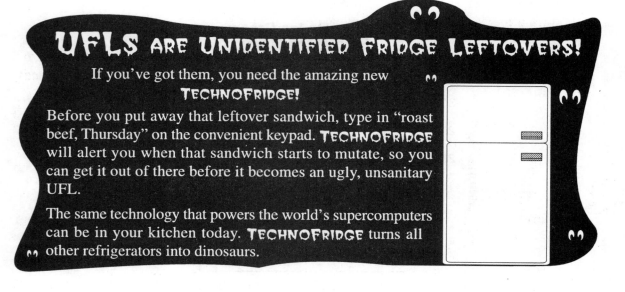

**UFLS ARE UNIDENTIFIED FRIDGE LEFTOVERS!**

If you've got them, you need the amazing new
**TECHNOFRIDGE!**

Before you put away that leftover sandwich, type in "roast beef, Thursday" on the convenient keypad. **TECHNOFRIDGE** will alert you when that sandwich starts to mutate, so you can get it out of there before it becomes an ugly, unsanitary UFL.

The same technology that powers the world's supercomputers can be in your kitchen today. **TECHNOFRIDGE** turns all other refrigerators into dinosaurs.

 **PRACTICE ACTIVITY**

**Directions:** Use the advertisement to answer questions 11 and 12.

11. All of the following are examples of TECHNOFRIDGE's advertised features **except** that it —
    A. has a convenient keypad
    B. uses supercomputer technology
    C. alerts you when food begins to be unsafe
    D. is priced lower than other refrigerators

12. The ad states, "TECHNOFRIDGE turns all other refrigerators into dinosaurs." What does this mean?

    _____

    _____

## Use the guides on a map to help you read it.

Most maps provide you with the following guides:

A **compass**, which indicates North, East, South, and West.

A **scale**, which tells you what each unit on the map (such as one-half inch) represents in terms of actual miles (such as 50 miles).

A **legend**, which is the key to reading a particular map. It is usually boxed and tells you how to read symbols, such as road signs.

Maps often use **coordinates** to identify locations. Coordinates are usually shown along the vertical and horizontal axes of the map. Letters are used to mark one axis, and numbers are used to mark the other.

Any place on the map can be identified by a letter and number combination. For example, on the map below, the Spruce Mountain Resort is at F2.

## PRACTICE ACTIVITY

**Directions**: Use the map at the right to answer questions 13–15.

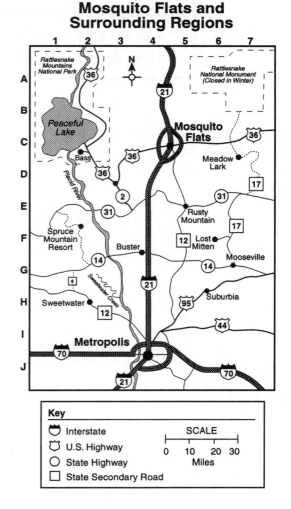

**Mosquito Flats and Surrounding Regions**

13. The road from Mosquito Flats to Peaceful Lake is classified as —
    A. an interstate highway
    B. a United States highway
    C. a state highway
    D. a state secondary road

14. The distance by road between Mosquito Flats and Metropolis is about how many miles?
    A. 30
    B. 40
    C. 90
    D. 120

15. If you took secondary road 12 south from Rusty Mountain, which direction should you turn to get to Buster?
    A. West on state highway 14
    B. West on state highway 310
    C. East on state highway 14
    D. East on state highway 310

### TIP #5  Read directions slowly, carefully, and in order.

Questions based on following directions usually look really easy. Since they look easy, it's very tempting to speed through them. But you know what happens when you're in a hurry—your chances of making a mistake go way up. So **slow down**, and double-check your work.

The best thing to do with a set of directions is to underline **order words** like "before," "then," and "after" that tell you when one thing happens in relation to another. Answer choices for directions questions often contain order words. They are very important.

Read through the directions as if you were actually going to perform the steps. This strategy will help you answer questions that require the **application** of information to a specific situation.

## Summing Up

As you answer questions about functional print, keep in mind the following tips:

- Know how to identify and read a table.
- Learn the different kinds of graphs and their purposes.
- Identify persuasive techniques in advertisements.
- Use the guides on a map to help you read it.
- Read directions slowly, carefully, and in order.

## PRACTICE SELECTION

**Directions:** Read the selection and answer the questions that follow.

# *How to Make Cut Flowers Last*

1. Cut at the right time. The best time to cut flowers is in the morning, just after they have opened and before it gets too hot.

2. Use a sharp knife. Dull scissors may crush the stem rather than cut it.

3. Cut on the diagonal. This gives more surface area for the intake of water.

4. After you cut each flower, place it in a half-full bucket of cool water. When you have cut all the flowers you will need, transfer them to a vase half filled with water.

5. Change the water in your vase daily. Bacteria from the decaying plants will get into the water.

6. Re-cut the bottoms of the stems when you change the water. This removes the part of the stem most affected by bacteria in the water.

## Sample Directions Questions

**Directions:** Read each question and circle the letter of the correct answer.

1. You will need a vase for steps —
   A. 2 and 3
   B. 3–5
   C. 4–6
   D. 1–6

2. If you did not have a sharp knife, what would be the **best** tool to use to cut the flowers?
   A. Your fingernails
   B. The edge of a shovel
   C. A dull pair of scissors
   D. The blade of a sharp pair of scissors

3. Just after you cut a flower, you should —
   A. water the plant
   B. clean off the bacteria
   C. place it in a bucket of water
   D. change the water in the bucket

# Sample Visual Information Questions

**Directions:** Use the map to answer questions 4–6.

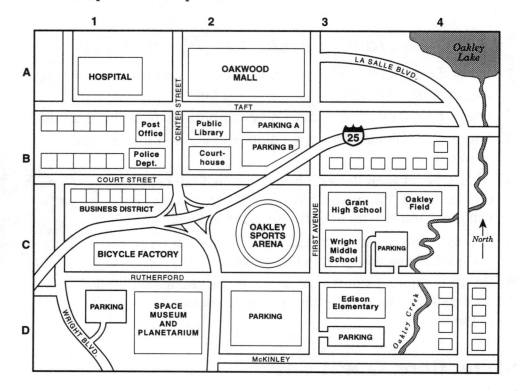

4. What building is located on the northwest corner of Center and Court Streets?
   A. Public Library
   B. Post Office
   C. Courthouse
   D. Police Department

5. To take the **most** direct route from the Space Museum parking lot to the Police Department, you would travel —
   A. east on Interstate 25, west on Court Street
   B. north on Wright Blvd., east on Court Street
   C. north on Wright Blvd., west on Rutherford
   D. east on Rutherford, north on First Avenue

6. Which two roads intersect at A4?
   A. Taft and La Salle Blvd.
   B. I-25 and Taft
   C. First Avenue and Taft
   D. First Avenue and La Salle Blvd.

**Directions:** Use the table to answer questions 7 and 8.

| Name | Department | Books Written | Years on Faculty |
|---|---|---|---|
| DeSoto | history | 2 | 7 |
| Sanchez | economics | 4 | 9 |
| Howard | English | 5 | 10 |
| Dexter | political science | 6 | 23 |
| Maxwell | chemistry | 9 | 22 |
| Davis | physics | 9 | 20 |

7. The names are listed in order based on —
   A. department
   B. books written
   C. alphabetical order
   D. years on faculty

8. Which person has been on the faculty longest?
   A. Sanchez
   B. Howard
   C. Davis
   D. Dexter

**Directions:** Use the circle graph to answer questions 9 and 10.

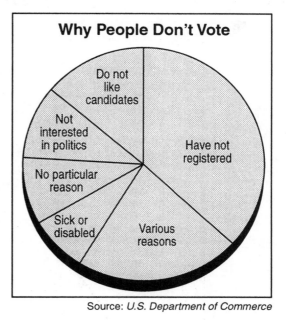

**Why People Don't Vote**

Do not like candidates

Not interested in politics

No particular reason

Sick or disabled

Various reasons

Have not registered

Source: *U.S. Department of Commerce*

9. What is the third largest single reason people gave for not voting?
   A. Do not like candidates
   B. Have not registered
   C. Not interested in politics
   D. Sick or disabled

10. If you were to convert this graph to a bar graph, you would have to find out how many —
   A. voters were polled
   B. voters are registered
   C. nonvoters were polled
   D. Americans are not registered

# unit 2

## In This Unit

Inference and Conclusion

Logical Relationships

Author's Purpose
and Viewpoint

# Critical Skills

Have you ever put a model airplane together or completed a jigsaw puzzle? In school, have you studied how the parts of the human body work together to create an individual body? If so, you've already learned and used critical skills.

Critical skills help you see how things work. Instead of just getting the "big picture" or looking at individual details, you can use critical skills to see how all the parts fit together. When you read, your critical skills help you understand connections among the details, the unstated ideas the author wants you to understand, and the author's purpose in writing the selection in the first place.

Practicing these skills will help you get inside a reading selection and see how the whole thing is put together.

# Lesson 5: Inference and Conclusion

One fine Friday afternoon, you rush home from school, ready to begin your weekend. Your family has just gotten a new parakeet, a bright yellow bird named Alice, who lives in a wire cage next to the bookshelf in the family room. You are looking forward to spending Saturday and Sunday getting acquainted with the bird.

You hurry up the front steps and into the family room, expecting to hear Alice's cheerful chirping, but you are puzzled by the strange silence. Alice's cage is where it's supposed to be, but Alice is nowhere in sight. The cage door is open.

You look around the room. All the windows are closed, so if she got out, she couldn't have gone far. At this point, you make an **inference**—a guess based on available information—about what has happened to Alice. You infer that she has escaped, and that she is somewhere in the house.

You decide to start searching for Alice. As you head toward the kitchen, your brother's cat, Elwood, scoots across the family room and into his favorite spot, a patch of afternoon sunlight beneath the picture window. You don't notice the single yellow feather sticking out of the corner of Elwood's mouth or the satisfied look on his face. If you did, you would probably come to a chilling **conclusion** about what happened to Alice.

Inferences and conclusions are reasonable guesses based on information you already know. The state test will ask you to make inferences and draw conclusions about the selections you read. The answers to these questions won't be directly stated in the selection. Your job is to be like a detective, piecing together the information you have read, getting a sense of the author's attitude, and determining the significance of the information.

**Directions:** Read the selection below. It will be used to explain the tips that follow.

## *United Through Language*
### by Gail Soerens

"I glad for freedom til I fool."
"If unna kyant behave unna self, I'll tek yu straight home."

The sentences above look something like the standard English most people in the United States speak today. If you repeat them a few times, you can probably figure out their meanings: "I was so glad to be free that I acted like a fool," and "If you can't behave yourself, I'll take you straight home." But notice that some of the words, grammar, and pronunciations are different from the kind of English spoken in most of the country today. That's because these sentences aren't exactly English. They are examples of Gullah, a mixture of English and West African languages.

Gullah was born of necessity. People forced into slavery were brought to North America from several African nations. The variety of languages spoken among them made communication difficult, yet they had a strong desire to overcome these difficulties, given their situation. Over time, thousands of words from various African languages became mixed with the English that the slaves were expected to know. The new language that resulted was called Gullah.

Gullah was the most common language of African Americans in South Carolina, Georgia, and neighboring areas during the years of slavery. It was an oral, rather than written, language; slaves were strictly forbidden to learn how to read or write, in any language. While the spellings of words vary, Gullah does have some basic rules or patterns of grammar. These were picked up as children listened to conversations and stories.

Many educated people have thought that Gullah is simply "uneducated" English. They have been convinced that the parts of Gullah that don't sound like English are mistakes made by people who had never gone to school. It wasn't until the 20th century that the African origins of Gullah were recognized and studied. Linguists now realize that Gullah is not "improper" English. It is a *creole language*—a common language created when people who speak different languages closely interact over a long time.

Over the past century, this hybrid language has became more and more like English. As more and more African Americans left their communities in the South to pursue new lives in the cities, the use of Gullah began to decline. A steady loss of oral culture has contributed to this decline.

Traces of Gullah still exist today, however. In fact, an estimated 250,000 people, most living in the isolated coastal marshes and sea islands of the Carolinas, Georgia, and northern Florida, speak a version of Gullah, although it is much closer to English than the Gullah spoken in the last century. There is also a Gullah cuisine, or type of cooking typical among these people.

Gullah has contributed such popular expressions as "chill out," "blow [one's] top," "geek," "zombie," "jazz," and "soulmate," to mainstream English. Its history should remind us of the importance of language in unifying a diverse people and of the creative power of the spoken word.

## TIP #1  Look for direct, but unstated, connections between details.

When answering an inference question, look for connections between the details. In many cases, inference questions are similar to implied cause and effect questions. Look for connections between details in the selection as you answer the next question.

1. Why do spellings of Gullah words vary?
   A. It is an oral, not a written, language.
   B. Those who speak Gullah are uneducated.
   C. Gullah is spoken today mostly in isolated regions.
   D. Over the past century, the use of Gullah has declined.

The selection addresses the issue of spelling (paragraph 3). The comment about spelling immediately follows a sentence that explains why Gullah was an oral, rather than a written, language. Things were not written in Gullah because slaves were not allowed to write.

### Read between the lines.

If your friend dislikes the way you've dressed (and she's a good enough friend to be honest with you), she may say, "Hey, you gonna tell me where I can get one of those outfits?" while raising her eyebrows, smirking, or rolling her eyes. Her body language says, "What possibly possessed you to dress *that way?*"

In order to read between the lines, it's important to pay attention to tone. As we discuss in Lesson 7, tone is like the "body language" of the author's "speech."

2. Is the author's tone toward the Gullah language mostly positive, negative, or neutral?

_____

3. The author gives the reader reason to think that —
    A. English has made an important contribution to the Gullah languages of Africa
    B. people should not speak Gullah if they don't want others to think they are uneducated
    C. Gullah became a way that slaves could communicate without their masters understanding them
    D. the hardship the Africans faced during enslavement contributed to their desire to communicate

The selection states, "The variety of languages spoken among them made communication difficult, yet there was a strong desire to overcome these difficulties, given their situation." That closing remark, "given their situation," is where you should "read between the lines." The author obviously means *something*, but is, for whatever reason, reluctant to spell it out. The idea that slaves faced "hardship" (D) is reasonable to assume, and it would certainly strengthen a desire to communicate with those in the same situation.

### Don't assume too much.

It is always possible to infer too much. Make sure that the conclusions you draw are reasonable *and* well supported by the given facts.

In number 3, choice C seems attractive to those who give some thought to the slaves' situation. It may well be true that slaves used Gullah to confuse their masters. There is, however, no suggestion in the selection that this was the case.

**Try to understand the purpose behind the offhand details the author presents.**

4. Why did the author mention Gullah cuisine?
    A. To encourage the reader to try Gullah food
    B. To explain the meaning of the word *cuisine*
    C. To show that the word *Gullah* describes more than just a language
    D. To compare the origins of Gullah food with the origins of the Gullah language

The idea that *Gullah* describes a whole culture, of which language is only a part, relates directly to the main idea of the selection by helping the reader better understand this key term.

**Identify the underlying questions answered in the selection.**

One trick to improving your reading is to be more conscious of the questions that arise in your mind. In conversation, it's easy. If your father tells you about a legendary baseball player who played for his favorite team while he was growing up, you might ask, "How often did you go to watch him play?"; "Did you ever meet him?"; "Is he still alive?" The same process applies to reading.

When reading narratives, your questions at first might be as simple as "What in the world will happen next?" Simply by asking this question, you focus your mind. Asking questions makes the details sink in and lessens the chance that your mind will wander as you're reading.

Answer the following question about the selection "United Through Language":

5. Which question is answered in the selection?
    A. What are some examples of Gullah speech?
    B. What are the rules of the Gullah language?
    C. What are some other examples of creole languages?
    D. Which African languages form the basis of Gullah?

By the way, asking questions as you go is also a good strategy for research and writing, as well. What do you really want to know? What does your reader want to know? If these questions are on your mind, you are guaranteed to make your writing more interesting and vivid.

## Summing Up

As you answer questions about inferences and conclusions, keep in mind the following tips:

- Look in the question for words that tell you to make an inference.

- Look for direct, but unstated, connections between details.

- Read between the lines.

- Don't assume too much.

- Try to understand the purpose behind the details.

- Identify the underlying questions answered by the selection.

© 1999 Buckle Down Publishing Company. DO NOT DUPLICATE.

**PRACTICE SELECTION**

**Directions:** Read the selection and answer the questions that follow.

from
## *The Moustache*
by Robert Cormier

*Mike is a high school senior whose grandmother lives in Lawnrest, a nursing home. He and his sister had planned to go there to visit her.*

At the last minute Annie couldn't go. She was invaded by one of those twenty-four-hour flu bugs that sent her to bed with a fever, moaning about the fact that she'd also have to break her date with Handsome Harry Arnold that night. We call him Handsome Harry because he's actually handsome, but he's also a nice guy, cool, and he doesn't treat me like Annie's kid brother, which I am, but like a regular person. Anyway, I had to go to Lawnrest alone that afternoon. But first of all I had to stand inspection. My mother lined me up against the wall. She stood there like a one-man firing squad, which is kind of funny because she's not like a man at all, she's very feminine, and we have this great relationship—I mean, I feel as if she really likes me. I realize that sounds strange, but I know guys whose mothers love them and cook special stuff for them and worry about them and all but there's something missing in their relationship.

Anyway. She frowned and started the routine.

"That hair," she said. Then admitted: "Well, at least you combed it."

I sighed. I have discovered that it's better to sigh than argue.

"And that moustache." She shook her head. "I still say a seventeen-year-old has no business wearing a moustache."

"It's an experiment," I said. "I just wanted to see if I could grow one." To tell the truth, I had proved my point about being able to grow a decent moustache, but I also had learned to like it.

"It's costing you money, Mike," she said.

"I know, I know."

The money was a reference to the movies. The Downtown Cinema has a special Friday night offer—half-price admission for high school couples, seventeen or younger. But the woman in the box office took one look at my moustache and charged me full price. Even when I showed her my driver's license. She charged full admission for Cindy's ticket, too, which left me practically broke and unable to take Cindy out for a hamburger with the crowd afterward. That didn't help matters, because Cindy has been getting impatient recently about things like the fact that I don't own my own car and have to concentrate on my studies if I want to win that college scholarship, for instance. Cindy wasn't exactly crazy about the moustache, either.

Now it was my mother's turn to sigh.

"Look," I said, to cheer her up. "I'm thinking about shaving it off." Even though I wasn't. Another discovery: You can build a way of life on postponement.

"Your grandmother probably won't even recognize you," she said. And I saw the shadow fall across her face.

# Sample Inference and Conclusion Questions

**Directions:** Read each question and circle the letter of the correct answer.

1. Based on the first paragraph of the selection, one could say that the relationship between Mike and his mother is —
   A. tense
   B. friendly
   C. carefree
   D. humorous

2. Based on the selection, one can conclude that —
   A. Mike's mother doesn't like his hairstyle
   B. Annie doesn't really like Handsome Harry
   C. Cindy doesn't want Mike to win a scholarship
   D. Cindy and Mike have been dating for a long time

3. Based on the selection, one could say that Mike likes wearing a moustache because —
   A. it causes girls to notice him
   B. his mother says she doesn't like it
   C. he likes it and thinks it looks good
   D. it makes him more attractive to Cindy

4. Based on paragraph 9, one can conclude that —
   A. Mike looks like he is older than seventeen
   B. the woman in the ticket booth knows Mike well
   C. Mike has a moustache on his driver's license picture
   D. a lot of other high school boys in Mike's town wear moustaches

5. After reading this selection, one can conclude that —
   A. Mike's mother is not a very good cook
   B. Lawnrest is about an hour's drive from Mike's house
   C. Annie is pretending to be sick to avoid going to Lawnrest
   D. Mike isn't really thinking about shaving off his moustache

6. What does Mike's mother mean when she says, "I still say a seventeen-year-old has no business wearing a moustache"?

   _____

   _____

   _____

   _____

   _____

   _____

# Additional Practice Questions

**Directions:** Now answer some other types of questions about the reading selection. You can learn about these question types in other lessons of this book.

7. In paragraph 2, what is the most likely cause of Mike's mother's frown?
   A. Concern about Annie's health
   B. Mike's lack of sympathy for Annie
   C. Thoughts about Mike's appearance
   D. Something Mike doesn't know about

8. Which of the following events is most likely to occur next in the story?
   A. Annie will suddenly feel better
   B. Mike will visit his grandmother
   C. Mike will purchase an automobile
   D. Cindy and Mike will have an argument

# Lesson 6: Logical Relationships

People usually choose their friends because they have something in common. Maybe they like the same kind of jokes. They might like the same kind of clothes, play the same sports, or enjoy the same type of music. Or they might just find that they think about things the same way. Somehow, the friendship just makes sense.

The friendship may be a "logical relationship," but that's not the kind of "relationship" that is meant in the title of this lesson. On the state test, some questions will ask you to understand the clearly stated or implied relationships between important details in a selection.

**Directions:** Read the autobiographical selection below. It will be used to explain the tips that follow.

from
## *The Great Flood of '55*
by Tom Fitzpatrick

The wind outside was howling.

I rolled over in bed and tried to slip into a sweet daydream, hoping to squeeze out a few more minutes of bliss.

But duty was calling. I had a paper route waiting. Thirty-six customers wanted their daily news over morning coffee. The luminous hands of the clock read 6:05. I hopped out of bed and got dressed.

*Ssh!* I didn't want to wake my brothers, Tommy and Donald, who slept in the next room. Actually, we slept in one long hall of a room in the attic of our home in Germantown. My side of the room was separated from theirs by a chimney. I had moved over to this back section after I graduated from sixth grade. I felt I deserved a room of my own, and this was the closest I could get.

It was hot and stuffy. An exhaust fan stuck in a little 2' x 2' window sucked out the oppressive air, but there was little circulation, since I kept the door closed to the mysterious back room of the attic. My parents used the back room to store their junk, but I was convinced that evil spirits lurked in its musty shadows. To tell the truth, I was afraid of the dark.

Outside, wind raged against our rooftop, but I couldn't hear the patter of rain. It had rained six out of the last nine days—hard, destructive rain that sent everyone scurrying for shelter. Two hurricanes, back to back, had battered our New England coast.

Downstairs, I could hear murmurs. My father must be up. He was an early riser, like myself. I liked nothing better than to get up early and share the kitchen table with Dad. He and I alone in the early morning hours— a pleasurable thought.

My Dad was not alone. I tiptoed downstairs to find him and Uncle Jimmy huddled in conference. They were business partners—they owned a dry cleaning plant on Main Street. What was Uncle Jimmy doing at our house?

I heard Uncle Jimmy say, "Waterbury's flooded. They're calling out the National Guard."

And my father asked, "What's it like downtown?"

"The river's going over its banks any time now. If we hurry, we can raise all the clothes to the ceiling. There's not much we can do about the equipment."

"Are we insured?"

"For floods? I . . . think so." My uncle's voice had an uncertain tone.

A flood in our valley! I was shocked. It seemed impossible. I went into the kitchen and made a slice of toast, covering it with peanut butter. I just couldn't believe that dirty little river could flood . . .

I had to deliver my papers, but I wanted to see the river first. I knew just where to go—the top of the sand bank behind my house. There I could look at the whole of my small town—downtown Main Street, with the highway heading north and south, and the river beside it, with all its angry fury.

I love great vistas, especially ones that show me familiar places. I am given a greater view of a smaller place, and my imagination soars. Vistas make the ordinary seem grand. Even Germantown seemed beautiful when seen from that high place. In truth, Germantown was sort of shabby, made up of struggling Polish, Italian, and Irish families, with no grand landmarks except for the three-story Polish-American hall that stood at the end of Beacon Street.

I rushed outside and ran to the top of the sand bank. It had stopped raining, but clouds hung so low I felt like I could almost touch them, and they were moving fast across the sky. The ground was soft and mushy under my feet, and for a second I thought the bank would cave in underneath me, sending me tumbling the hundred feet to the bottom.

There I saw the river, galloping its way south. Normally this little cesspool of a stream hardly made a dent in the panorama. Yet there it was, making a wide turn around the state highway garage and threatening to overrun its banks behind the community center. Amazing!

The river looked angry, as if it were seeking revenge for all the crimes committed against it. We had taken the river for granted, and now the river was getting even.

### Look for words that show a cause and effect relationship.

As you're reading a selection, you may come across words or phrases that make it clear you're dealing with a cause and effect relationship. Not all cause and effect relationships are revealed by specific words, but looking for such words can be a good place to start.

Read the item below:

1. According to paragraph 5, the narrator's room lacked circulation because –
   A. he kept a small fan in his window
   B. his parents had stuffed it full of junk
   C. he kept the door to the back room closed
   D. he thought evil spirits lurked in the attic

The selection says that "There was little circulation, *since* I kept the door closed to the mysterious back room of the attic." The word *since* tells you a cause and effect relationship is being described between the closed door and the lack of circulation.

In addition, several other words and phrases can tip you off to cause and effect relationships. Some examples are shown below:

| | | | |
|---|---|---|---|
| because of | increased/decreased | so | produced |
| resulted in | as a consequence of | hence | thus |
| in order to | was responsible for | led to | caused |
| in response to | due to | affected | |

 **Look for unstated cause and effect relationships based on the logic of the text.**

Not all cause and effect relationships are described using the words listed in Tip 1. Often, it's up to the reader to make the connection. One way to do this is to create a because sentence that links two events. To practice this tip, complete the following sentence:

2. The narrator had to get out of bed **because**

_____

Now answer the following question:

3. The narrator had to get out of bed in order to –
   A. deliver newspapers
   B. wake his brothers
   C. have breakfast with his father
   D. help fight back the flood waters

## *Infer* cause and effect relationships *implied* by the author.

What if you think you've found a cause and effect relationship, but you can't find a cause and effect tip-off word or even two sentences you could hitch with a *because*? This doesn't mean you don't have a cause and effect relationship. It may just mean the author has hinted at a cause and effect relationship and counted on you to figure it out yourself.

4. Uncle Jimmy was at the narrator's house because —
   A. he sought immediate help from the narrator's father
   B. he wanted to have breakfast with the narrator's father
   C. he wanted to start a dry cleaning business with the narrator's father
   D. he wanted to ask the narrator's father if the business was insured against floods

## Problems and solutions are another kind of cause and effect relationship.

Finding the solution to a problem or finding what problem was solved by a certain action is a lot like identifying causes and effects. These problem and solution questions might look something like the following:

5. What does Uncle Jimmy suggest as a solution to the possibility of water entering the dry cleaning plant?
   A. Sandbagging the river
   B. Raising the clothes to the ceiling
   C. Insuring the dry-cleaning equipment
   D. Asking the help of the National Guard

## Look for words that show a comparison/contrast relationship.

Words such as *like*, *as*, *both*, *unlike*, and *but* can clue you in to logical relationships in which either similarity or difference is established. Pay attention to the logic of these words when you encounter them in the text.

6. One way the narrator and his father are **alike** is that —
   A. both like vistas
   B. both enjoy breakfast
   C. both sleep in the attic
   D. both are early risers

Here is a chart of several words and phrases that can tip you off to a comparison/contrast relationship.

| Comparison Words | Contrast Words |
|---|---|
| like | unlike |
| same | different |
| similar to | as opposed to |
| both | only |
| as much as | more than |
| just as | not at all like |
| equally | unequally |

**Use your senses—and your imagination—to make what you're reading "come alive."**

Many comparisons are made based on sensory detail: two things look, sound, smell, taste, or feel the same or different. Use your five senses when you are reading to imagine the details that are presented. They will help you experience what the reading selection is about. Comparisons or contrasts stated or implied in the selection will become concrete and memorable through your imagination.

7. What is the difference between the "dirty little river" the narrator knows and the "galloping river" it has become?

   A. The river was dirty, but it has become much more clear.

   B. The river seemed insignificant, but it has become a powerful force.

   C. The river was quick-moving, but it has become large and ponderous.

   D. The river had a bad reputation, but now it has earned that reputation.

## Look for comparisons made using figures of speech.

Figures of speech help the reader understand an unfamiliar thing or event by comparing it to something more familiar. They can also add interest to a story or poem. Similes, metaphors, and personification are important figures of speech. (You can learn more about these in Lesson 9.) Again, the best way to understand their logic is to "experience" the comparison being made. Then try to identify what the two things being compared have in common.

8. How is the river similar to a person who is angry or seeks revenge?
   A. It is swollen and muddy.
   B. It is making a loud howling sound.
   C. It is behaving with unusual violence.
   D. It has risen almost even with the village.

## Summing Up

When answering questions about logical relationships, remember the following tips:

- Look for words that show cause and effect relationships.
- Look for unstated relationships based on the logic of the text.
- Infer unstated cause and effect relationships.
- Problems and solutions are another type of cause and effect relationship.
- Look for words that show a comparison/contrast relationship.
- Use your senses and your imagination to make what you're reading "come alive."
- Look for comparisons made using figures of speech.

▶ **PRACTICE SELECTION**

**Directions:** Read the selection and answer the questions that follow.

adapted from
# *To Build a Fire*
by Jack London

And then it happened. At a place where there were no signs, where the soft, unbroken snow seemed to advertise solidity beneath, the man broke through. It was not deep. He wet himself halfway to the knees before he floundered out to the firm crust.

He was angry, and cursed his luck aloud. He had hoped to get into camp with the boys at six o'clock, and this would delay him an hour, for he would have to build a fire and dry out his footgear. This was imperative at that low temperature—he knew that much; and he turned aside to the bank, which he climbed. On top, tangled in the underbrush about the trunks of several small spruce trees, was a high-water deposit of dry firewood—sticks and twigs, principally, but also larger portions of seasoned branches and fine, dry grasses. He threw down several large pieces on top of the snow. This served as a foundation and prevented the young flame from drowning itself in the snow it otherwise would melt. . . .

He worked slowly and carefully, keenly aware of his danger. When it is seventy-five below zero, a man must not fail in his first attempt to build a fire— that is, if his feet are wet. If his feet are dry, and he fails, he can run along the trail for half a mile and restore his circulation. But the circulation of wet and freezing feet cannot be restored by running when it is seventy-five below. No matter how fast he runs, the wet feet will freeze all the harder.

All this the man knew. The old-timer on Sulphur Creek had told him about it the previous fall, and now he was appreciating the advice. Already all sensation had gone out of his feet. To build the fire, he had been forced to remove his mittens, and the fingers had quickly gone numb. . . .

The fire was beginning to burn with strength. He was feeding it with twigs the size of his finger. In another minute he would be able to feed it with branches the size of his wrist, and then he could remove his

The life of **Jack London** (1876–1916) was as adventure-filled as his writing. His year in the Alaskan Klondike turned up something more valuable than gold: the "raw material" upon which he based stories like this one.

wet footgear, and, while it dried, he could keep his naked feet warm by the fire, rubbing them at first, of course, with snow. The fire was a success. He was safe. He remembered the advice of the old-timer on Sulphur Creek, and smiled. The old-timer had been very serious in laying down the law that no man must travel alone in the Klondike after fifty below.

Well, here he was. He had had the accident, he was alone, and he had saved himself. All a man had to do was keep his head, and he was all right. Any man could travel alone. But it was surprising, the rapidity with which his cheeks and nose were freezing. And he had not thought his fingers could go lifeless in so short a time. When he touched a twig, he had to look and see whether or not he had hold of it. The wires were pretty well down between him and his fingertips.

All of which counted for little. There was the fire, snapping and crackling and promising life with every dancing flame. He started to untie his moccasins. They were coated with ice. The thick German socks were like sheaths of iron halfway to the knees; the moccasin strings were like rods of steel, all twisted and knotted. For a moment he tugged with his numb fingers, then, realizing the folly of it, he drew his sheath knife.

But before he could cut the strings, it happened. It was his own fault, or rather, his mistake. He should not have built the fire under the spruce tree. He should have built it in the open. But it had been easier to pull the twigs from the brush and drop them directly on the fire. Now the tree under which he had done this carried a weight of snow on its boughs. No wind had blown for weeks, and each bough was fully <u>freighted</u>. Each time he had pulled a twig, he had communicated a slight agitation to the tree, sufficient to bring about the disaster. High up in the tree one bough capsized its load of snow. This fell on the boughs beneath, capsizing them. This process continued, spreading out and involving the whole tree. It grew like an avalanche, and it descended without warning upon the man and the fire, and the fire was blotted out! Where it had burned was a mantle of fresh and disordered snow.

# Sample Logical Relationships Questions

**Directions:** Read each question and circle the letter of the correct answer.

1. The man knows what to do in the Klondike because he —
   A. has often traveled in the Klondike region
   B. learned from an old-timer on Sulphur Creek
   C. once met another traveler building a fire along the way
   D. practiced Klondike survival skills when he was in the camp

2. In paragraph 7, the man draws his sheath knife in order to —
   A. ward off an animal attack
   B. cut twigs to put on the fire
   C. cut the frozen laces of his shoes
   D. break through the ice to get water

3. What was the **main** cause of the man's fire being blotted out?
   A. The wind suddenly begins to blow.
   B. A snow-laden tree collapses onto the fire.
   C. An avalanche comes down the mountain.
   D. Snow from overhead branches falls on the fire.

4. Which solution might solve the man's problem?
   A. Running to camp
   B. Starting another fire
   C. Rubbing his feet with snow
   D. Sitting and waiting for help

# Additional Practice Questions

**Directions:** Now answer some other types of questions about the reading selection. You can learn about these question types in other lessons of this book.

5. How cold is it in the Klondike when the story takes place?
   A. 6 degrees below zero
   B. 50 degrees below zero
   C. 75 degrees below zero
   D. 90 degrees below zero

6. The **first** problem the man faces in the story is that —
   A. a fire he is building goes out
   B. his feet and fingers get numb
   C. he gets wet halfway to the knees
   D. he must stop to remove his footgear

7. When the author says, "The wires were pretty well down between him and his fingertips," he means that —
   A. the man's fingers no longer work very well
   B. the man has no way to call anyone for help
   C. the man is trying to untie the knots in his shoelaces
   D. the man's fingers are no longer connected to his body

8. Which sentence is the **best** summary of "To Build a Fire"?
   A. A hiker has an accident while traveling to a camp.
   B. A man starts a fire to keep himself warm in the Klondike.
   C. A man goes hiking in the Klondike on an extremely cold day.
   D. A lone hiker in the Klondike tries to build a fire to keep from freezing.

9. In this selection, the word *freighted* means —
   A. loaded
   B. frozen
   C. broken
   D. visible

# Lesson 7: Author's Purpose and Viewpoint

You've probably heard people talk about something called "body language." We use body language to give people messages about ourselves—our moods, attitudes, and opinions. Body language speaks for us without our ever saying a word. It also tells people whether or not we really mean what we say.

Writers have a way of speaking to us that is a lot like body language. Sure, sometimes they'll directly say, "I don't like this." But just as often they try to tell the reader what they think without coming right out and saying so. And sometimes they'll show us that there's more to their message than we can see at first glance.

You can learn how writers feel about a topic—their points of view—by looking carefully at the words they use. Are the words glowingly positive? Extremely negative? Pretty much neutral? Writers' words are clues that can lead you to discover their purpose for writing, which is important in evaluating what you read.

**To determine an author's point of view, begin with "pro," "con," and neutral.**

Many authors begin with a simple "pro" (for) or "con" (against) stance on a subject, then develop their reasons for being "pro" or "con" later. As a reader, you should be able to spot their obvious biases. Other authors set out to offer a neutral view of a subject, weighing the different sides rather than stating a position.

**Directions:** Read this excerpt from a music review and answer the questions that follow.

## *LeAnn Rimes*

by Greta Anderson

What can you say about a girl who has sold more than nine million records, paid for a new home for her family, and won two Grammy Awards by the age of 14? People are speechless about the success of the young country singer, LeAnn Rimes, but they're even more impressed by the quality of her voice. LeAnn has never taken voice lessons but says that she's been singing all her life, and she still loves to sing: "I sing in the shower, in the car. I've been told I actually sing in my sleep." When she sings, you want to say, "perfect," but it's more than that.

LeAnn is almost speechless about her success, as well. When she looks at her career, she says, one word sums it up: "Crazy."

Of course, hearing that word, your mind turns to the familiar strains of a song Patsy Cline popularized. Except this time you hear Rimes's fresher, sweeter version of it, and you know that it's happened to you. You've become enthralled by her power of song.

1.  Is the author's opinion of LeAnn Rimes positive, negative, or neutral?

    _____

    _____

2.  You can tell from the selection that the author —
    A. wants to judge LeAnn Rimes fairly
    B. prefers Patsy Cline to LeAnn Rimes
    C. believes LeAnn Rimes is a great singer
    D. dislikes LeAnn Rimes's style of singing

It is a good idea to ask yourself *where* this review might be printed. In a teen magazine? Well, those magazines thrive on hype. What if it's printed on the CD jacket or comes as part of a promotional mailing? In that case, it deserves to be called **propaganda**. Propaganda is writing that takes extreme measures to influence the reader's behavior— in this case, the purchase of Rimes's CDs.

 **Understand the four basic purposes for writing.**

An author's purpose for writing influences not only *what* is written but *how* it is written. The writer's purpose will almost always fall into one of four major categories: to persuade, to describe, to entertain, or to inform.

**Writing to Persuade**
Persuasive writing is designed to make the reader think, believe, or act the same way the author does. If the topic is a serious issue—pollution, crime, or other dangers— the author might try to alarm the reader with predictions of harm. Authors might also encourage people to do something in response to their ideas, such as vote for a candidate, boycott a business, or recycle tin cans. Persuasion selections are usually filled with opinions. If there are two or more sides to an issue, the writer presents one of them as being the best. Newspaper editorials and most advertisements are written to persuade.

A piece of writing becomes propaganda when the author uses half-truths or falsehoods, name calling, or other extreme measures to get the reader to think or behave in a certain way. It's up to the reader to decide what is a fair argument based on well-reasoned opinions, and what is sheer propaganda.

**Writing to Describe**
By now, you're very familiar with writing that is designed to teach. School texts and workbooks (such as this one) are prime examples. Others include "how-to" books and magazines, recipes, and instructions.

**Writing to Entertain**
Your favorite authors are probably those who write to entertain. Most works of fiction, such as novels, short stories, and comic books, are designed to entertain.

## Writing to Inform

The best examples of informational writing are news stories on the front page of your daily newspaper and nonfiction articles in magazines. The purpose of this kind of writing is to provide factual information in a balanced manner. If there are two sides to an issue, the writer presents both and lets the readers draw their own conclusions.

**Directions:** Read the selection below and use it as you study some more tips on author's purpose.

adapted from

# *The Old Spotted Dog*

by Will Rogers

While I didn't have anything else to do, I got to watching an old spotted dog. He was just an ordinary dog, but when I looked at him close, he was alert and friendly with everyone. I got to inquiring around and found he'd been bumped off a freight train and seemed to have no owner. He made himself at home and started right in business. When a crowd of cowboys would go into a diner, he would follow 'em in and begin entertaining. He could do all kinds of tricks—turn somersaults, lay down and roll over, sit up on his hind feet, and such like.

> **Will Rogers** was born in Oklahoma in 1879. This part-Cherokee, full-blooded cowboy was known and loved by the whole nation for his good-humored, plain-speaking observations of politics, news, and human nature. The events of "The Old Spotted Dog" date back to when Will Rogers worked as a cowboy near Amarillo, Texas, at the tender age of eighteen.

He would always rush to the door and shake hands with all the newcomers. The boys would lay a coin on his nose, and he'd toss it high in the air and catch it in his mouth and pretend to swallow it. But you could bet your life he didn't swallow it—he stuck it in one side of his lip and when he got a lip full of money, he'd dash out the back door and disappear for a few minutes. What he really done was hide his money. As soon as he worked one saloon, he would pull out and go to another place.

I got to thinking while watching this old dog, how much smarter he is than me. Here I am out of a job five hundred miles from home, and sitting around and can't find a thing to do, and this old dog hops off a train and starts right in making money, hand over fist.

Me and some boys around town tried to locate his hidden treasure, but this old dog was too slick for us. He never fooled away no time on three or four of us boys that was looking for work. He seemed to know we was broke, but he was very friendly. As he was passing along by me, he'd wag his tail and kind of wink. I must have looked hungry and forlorn. I think he wanted to buy me a meal.

When times was dull and he got hungry, he would mysteriously disappear.
Pretty soon he'd show up at a butcher shop with a dime in his mouth and lay
it on the counter and the butcher would give him a piece of steak or a bone.
He always paid for what he got in the line of grub. Pretty soon he seemed to
get tired of the town, and one morning he was gone. A railroad man told us
later that he'd seen this same dog in Trinidad, Colorado.

3. The author's purpose in this selection is to —
   A. describe someone's pet
   B. convince the reader to purchase a dog
   C. tell the reader about the Depression years
   D. amuse the reader with an unbelievable yarn

The "purpose" words have been changed, but they're still the same four. *Tell* is another
word for *inform, convince* is another word for *persuade,* and *amuse* is another word
for *entertain.* You may well encounter these synonyms on the test.

If the selection stopped halfway through the second paragraph, we could believe in
this performing dog. The rest is entertaining fiction, and Rogers only hopes the reader
lets out a chuckle.

### Identify the mood of the writing.

If a friend complains to you about all the chores his parents make him do around the
house, he's probably trying to get you to feel sorry for him. A writer tells you all
sorts of details in order to make you feel something. He or she uses these feelings
to develop a **mood**.

Mood is particularly important in narratives. It can be established by describing
the setting, the characters and their feelings, the action, or a combination of those
elements. The writer may develop a mood of suspense, violence, humor, seriousness,
peacefulness, danger, sorrow, sarcasm, fear, happiness—or a host of other emotions.

Now let's try the same question with more subtle answer choices. The selection is
not "just" a tall tale. Every narrative has a kernel of truth to reveal, no matter how
silly the story may be. Look again at the details of the selection and the sidebar
to determine what "real story" they have to tell.

4. One of the author's purposes in this selection is to —
   A. recall a friendly dog he once owned
   B. show how pathetic a person without a job can be
   C. provide a model for young men who are out of a job
   D. poke fun at the struggles he faced early in his career

**Decide where the writing most likely would appear.**

If the selection is neutral and filled with information, it might appear in an encyclopedia or a news article. If the selection is intended to persuade readers on an issue, or provide light observations on local topics, it could very well appear in the editorial section of a newspaper. Fiction pieces are usually found in books or magazines.

5.  In which source would you be most likely to find "The Old Spotted Dog"?
    A.  A collection of tall tales
    B.  A history of Amarillo, Texas
    C.  A magazine about dog training
    D.  An encyclopedia article about Rogers

## Summing Up

As you try to identify the purpose behind an author's writing, keep these things in mind:

- To determine an author's point of view, begin with "pro," "con," and neutral.
- Understand the four basic purposes for writing.
- Identify the mood of the writing.
- Decide where the writing most likely would appear.

### PRACTICE SELECTION 1

**Directions:** Read the selections and answer the questions that follow.

# If You Win, I Lose? – Get Lost!

### by Marie McDonald

From the time I was a youngster, I have been something of a klutz. My athletic prowess will never win me medals. Jump-ropes have a way of snaring me like a rabbit caught in a trap or slapping me on the cheek just to keep me in my place. The last time I played softball, I caught a fly—right between the eyes. Just the other day my son shot a basket over me and the descending ball rebounded off my skull. I seem to be hopeless at athletic competition, and I have learned to avoid it at all costs.

Maybe my klutziness explains why I despise competitive games. How can a person spend a lifetime being the last one chosen without feeling put down and generally worthless? I had other abilities. I got good grades. I had the lead in the school play. I could ride my bike with no hands. Did any of these things matter to my self-image or to my standing in the school community? Very little, I'm afraid. The truth is, in my school, if you couldn't catch an infield fly (with your glove, not your face), if you couldn't make a lay-up or a freethrow, or if you couldn't serve a volleyball, you weren't much of a social asset. When it came time for gym teams to chose sides, you were destined to feel like a lonely oddity from *Ripley's Believe It or Not.*

Although it seemed at the time that everyone but me won athletic contests and had medals to prove it, I've discovered that I was not alone. Several of my acquaintances still bear hidden scars from losing all (or at least most) of the time. Like me, they laughed at themselves and pretended their disgrace didn't matter. But it really did. I'm convinced that scars like these do little more than fade with time. For many of us, they never really disappear.

To prevent permanent embarrassment, I avoid competitive games. I'd rather go on a hike with my family, take a bike trip with friends, do aerobics in a fitness class, or try to beat my own time running at the local track. I don't need to triumph over someone else to feel like a winner. And I no longer allow myself to feel like a loser. After all, playing games is supposed to be about having fun, isn't it? So, if you want to use competition to prove your worth at my expense, please count me out.

 **PRACTICE SELECTION 2**

# *What Have You Got to Lose?*

by Jane Duncalf

Junior high can be a rather traumatic time for any teenager, and my experience was no exception. Not only was I the shortest person in my class, I was downright puny. In fact, I would say I looked about eight years old in the eighth grade. Of course this made for some good-natured teasing. It also made me feel totally inept at sports. (My classmates must have felt the same way about me—I *never* was picked for gym teams until last.) Even Red Rover games were a nightmare because everyone would try to run through the weakest link in the line—me. By the middle of eighth grade, I had pretty much given up all hope of gaining popularity through athletics.

Once I had accepted my ineptness at sports, it was easier to move on and look at competitive sports from a "this could be fun, I don't have to be good" perspective. With this in mind, I decided to participate in spring track. I had no grandiose visions of myself as a track star. All my friends were trying out and I thought it would be fun. As it turned out, I not only enjoyed myself, I also found my niche in sports. I continued to compete in track meets throughout high school.

I could easily have let my early bad experiences with competition keep me from trying out for sports. If I had, I'd have missed an experience that meant much more than a mere record of wins and losses. Track gave me a new-found confidence that I could be good at *something*. Did being a good runner make me feel accepted? No, but it did make me feel that I was a contributing member of a group. (I decided that I had been accepted by my peers long before, not for the number of track medals I could win, but for all of the inner strengths and weaknesses they had recognized in me over the years.) Competition brought us together, but it was the teamwork and team spirit growing out of it that made us a close-knit unit.

Working hard in practice, complaining about our aches and pains, goofing off, and cheering each other on resulted in a camaraderie that came from striving together to win. Our track team had its share of wins and losses, but this didn't seem to matter. No one—not even our coach—got mad if one of us tripped and lost our race or dropped a baton. I can only remember words of encouragement from teammates who would be there at the end of the race to pat our runners on the back, even if they came in dead last. Sure, we wanted to win, and we all tried individually to be successful for the team. In doing so, we shared the special closeness that comes with working together to accomplish a mutual goal. Whether or not we actually won didn't mean nearly as much, nor do I remember it as vividly, as the fun we had trying.

I also remember the friendly rivalries between individual runners who competed against each other year after year. I always had a rival from another team whom I really wanted to beat. Before a race, we would talk about our best times for the season, usually trying to "psych each other out." It never really worked—everyone was going to give it their best, no matter what anyone else said. At the end of every race, regardless of who won or lost, my competitors and I shared exhausted hugs and congratulations. Sometimes I won, but when I didn't, the loss gave me a real respect for the other person's talent and challenged me to work harder.

Participating in competitive sports may not be for everyone, but it's important to try to find something that you care enough about to be willing to risk some ups and downs. There will probably be a little competition involved in almost anything you attempt, whether it's seeking a part in a school play, running for student government, applying for a job, writing for the school paper, or entering an art show. Speaking from my own experiences, the best approach to competition may be to focus on finding something you really enjoy doing. Once you find your niche, you may find that competition isn't all about winning and losing. The real value of competition may be in the opportunities it provides to improve yourself, pursue your goals, work with others—and have fun. What have you got to lose?

# Sample Author's Purpose Questions

**Directions:** Read each question and circle the letter of the correct answer or write your response on the lines provided.

1. What is the author's **main** purpose in writing selection 1?
   A. To strongly protest all sporting activities
   B. To make fun of anyone who isn't very athletic
   C. To describe the negative effects of competition
   D. To amuse the reader with stories from her childhood

2. What is the author's **main** purpose in writing paragraph 1 of selection 1?
   A. To ridicule herself
   B. To report facts about her life
   C. To provide support for her viewpoint
   D. To entertain those who agree with her

3. What is the author's **main** purpose in writing selection 2?
   A. To illustrate the importance of athletic skill
   B. To convince others that competition has benefits
   C. To encourage others to compete in high school track
   D. To gain recognition for her athletic accomplishments

4. What is the author's **main** purpose in writing paragraph 1 of selection 2?
   A. To vent feelings of anger at her mistreatment
   B. To provide a background for her view on sports
   C. To gain sympathy for being teased about her size
   D. To explain why she lacks confidence in her athletic ability

5. Which word **best** describes the overall tone selection 1 takes toward competition?
   A. Critical
   B. Furious
   C. Satisfied
   D. Resigned

6. Which of the following **best** describes the overall tone of selection 2?
   A. Boastful and proud
   B. Critical and superior
   C. Competitive and driven
   D. Motivating and encouraging

7. Which sentence **best** describes the author's attitude toward the rivals mentioned in paragraph 5 of selection 2?
   A. You should take advantage of your rivals' weaknesses.
   B. Having rivals can help you to become a better competitor.
   C. As an athlete, you should do whatever it takes to beat your rivals.
   D. Beating your rivals by a large margin makes winning more satisfying.

8. Where are these selections **most likely** to appear?
   A. In an encyclopedia
   B. In a scholarly journal
   C. In a magazine editorial
   D. On a newspaper's front page

9. How do the two authors' attitudes about competition compare?

   _____

   _____

   _____

   _____

   _____

   _____

   _____

   _____

# Additional Practice Questions

**Directions**: Now answer some other types of questions about the reading selection. You can learn more about these question types in other parts of this book.

10. Read this quote.

> Maybe my klutziness explains why I despise competitive games. How can a person spend a lifetime being the last one chosen without feeling put down and generally worthless?

Which of the following phrases could **best** be used in place of the word *despise?*
A. Try hard at
B. Participate in
C. Don't understand
D. Intensely dislike

11. What is selection 1 **mainly** about?
A. The disadvantages of competition
B. The author's lack of athletic ability
C. The importance of athletics in modern life
D. The use of competition to prove a person's worth

12. According to the author of selection 1, why would a sport such as hiking be superior to a sport such as softball?
A. Softball can be dangerous.
B. Hiking gives a better workout.
C. Hiking has no winners or losers.
D. Softball requires special equipment.

13. Read this quote.

> Working hard in practice, complaining about our aches and pains, goofing off, and cheering each other on resulted in a camaraderie that came from striving together to win.

What does the word *camaraderie* mean?
A. Ability
B. Confidence
C. Satisfaction
D. Friendship

# unit 3

# Literary Skills

When we read a good story, we tend to get pulled into the world of the characters. Everything seems to fit together so naturally that we forget the whole thing is the work of an author who used specific techniques for creating that "natural" feel of the writing.

Actually, literary writing has just as many (and often more) levels of structure than informational writing. To fully understand a story or poem, you need to be familiar with the specific skills that will help you see the structure and meaning of literary works.

You'll learn the basic building blocks of a story and the special ways authors use language to appeal to your senses. This will help you get more out of not only stories and poems but also other types of writing that sometimes use these language tools.

# Lesson 8: Story Elements

It was a dark and stormy night. Inside the Victorian house she had just moved into, Julie stroked her nervous cat on a crushed velvet sofa. "Well, it's a dark and stormy night," Julie mumbled out loud. "I guess we'll find out just what kind of protection this house has to offer." A sudden flash of lightning, followed by thunder, caused her to add, in a quavering voice, "Won't we, Sissy?" The cat responded with a long, drawn-out growl, her tail swishing wildly from one side to the other. . . .

Once upon a time, long, long ago at the crest of a fertile valley leading to the sea, there lived a Viking lord and his family. Young men who had proven themselves in battle would come to the valley, hoping to make the lord's lovely daughter, Kristina, their bride. The lord and his wife made great shows of hospitality. But Kristina would take one look at her suitors and retire silently to her chamber. None of them matched the handsome man she had seen in that startling dream, over two years ago. . . .

The police found the body at 4:00 A.M., lying in a pool of blood. Arriving just forty-five minutes later, Detective Dick Stevens was a little gruff: Not only had his sleep been interrupted, but his morning training schedule would be thrown out of whack. The marathon was only thirteen days away. . . .

What will happen in these three stories? You can probably make a pretty accurate guess, just based on their opening paragraphs. That's because you already understand a lot about story structure and types of stories. When you were learning to talk, you picked up the basic patterns of speech because you heard them all the time. You've also picked up the basic patterns of narrative from repeated exposure to them.

## PRACTICE ACTIVITY

**Directions**: Okay, go for it. Write one sentence telling what you think will probably happen in the three stories above.

1. (Julie's house) _____

   _____

2. (The Viking maid, Kristina) _____

   _____

3. (Detective Dick Stevens) _____

   _____

**Learn about the different narrative genres.**

Part of knowing how these stories will develop depends on knowing the basic types, or **genres**, of fiction. The first excerpt is from a horror story, designed to raise the hairs on your arms. That's how you know that Julie's house will turn out to be a scary place. The second excerpt is from a fairy tale. That's how you know that Kristina will eventually meet the "man of her dreams." The third excerpt is from a mystery. That's how you know Detective Dick Sevens will find the murderer *and* run the marathon, and that somehow, those two things will be connected.

Important narrative genres include:

**Realistic fiction:** The story is believable; it could happen to anyone. The main character often faces an emotional or psychological conflict.

**Adventure stories:** Not much "psychological stuff" for these characters. It's one action scene after the next.

**Mysteries:** A crime is committed. In finding the criminal, a detective—the most fully-drawn character in the story—must unravel a web of clues before pinning down the suspect.

**Historical fiction:** The story is set in a specific time in history. These stories sometimes include actual historical figures.

**Science fiction:** The story is set in a time or place when technology has reshaped society in significant ways. The unusual setting often helps to highlight "human" dilemmas all the more.

**Tall tales:** Like "The Old Spotted Dog" by Will Rogers in Lesson 7, a tall tale is an ordinary story that has been stretched so far that it becomes ridiculously unbelievable.

**Learn about the "building blocks" of storytelling.**

Every narrative on the shelves of the library has been constructed out of the "building blocks" of storytelling. Each boils down to the statement: *Something happens to someone, somewhere.*

The "something" that happens is called the **plot** of the story. The "someone" to whom it happens (or who makes it happen) is a **character**. The character has some sort of problem, or **conflict**, that must be resolved in the course of the story. The "somewhere" is the **setting**, where and when the story takes place.

The setting, along with the author's purpose, creates the mood of the story, or the overall feeling the story creates for the reader.

**Follow the development of the plot.**

Aristotle, a philosopher who lived in ancient Greece, described the essence of fiction as "beginning, middle, and end." Things change over the course of a story; your initial judgments may be reversed as the plot thickens.

**Directions:** Read the selection below. It will be used to explain the tips that follow.

# *Slom Season*

adapted from *Mårbacka: The Story of a Manor*

by Selma Lagerlöf

East of Mårbacka, beyond a wooded ridge, lies a little lake in which there is a fish we call *slom*. The fish are about two inches long and so thin as to be almost transparent; but small as they are, these fish are edible.

When I was a little girl, folks used to take this fish out of the lake in countless numbers. Its spawning time was in early spring, when the ice began to break and there was open water along the shores. One could stand at the water's edge and scoop the fish up with dippers and buckets. Certainly no one went to the bother of putting out nets for slom!

Slom was fished and sold only at spawning time; therefore it was a sure sign of spring when a fisherman came to the kitchen at Mårbacka with the first catch. The man, knowing he had brought a desired commodity, boldly lifted the latch (in those days there were no knobs) and walked in with an air of confident assurance. He did not stop just inside the door as on other occasions, but without stating his errand or even saying good-morning, he strode across the floor to the big table and deposited a small plate of fish. Then, stepping back to the door, he stood proudly and waited for what was to follow.

If the housekeeper and maids were the only ones in the kitchen, he might stand a long while unnoticed, for they made a game out of not recognizing him. But as soon as we girls saw the plate, a sense of excitement took over. It was the same excitement we felt every winter with the first snowfall.

My father was such a lover of fish that he wouldn't eat anything else. All winter he had made do with dried pike and salted whitefish, to say nothing of the endless pickled herring! With the approach of slom season, he would ask every day whether the slom had arrived.

Aunt Louisa, who lived with us, might hear our excitement and join us in the kitchen. As soon as she caught sight of slom, she would throw up her hands and exclaim in despair, "Oh, heavens! Is that awful stuff coming in now again?"

*(To be continued . . .)*

> **Selma Lagerlöf** (1858–1940) was the first woman to receive the Nobel Prize for Literature. As a child growing up in Sweden, she loved to listen to the stories her grandmother would tell, and she decided to be a writer so that she could keep those stories alive. She grew up on a farm, called Mårbacka, that was always bustling with visitors.

**Get to know the characters through what they say and do.**

Already we have some initial sense of the two main characters. What kind of person would love slom so much that he would ask, every single day, whether it was in yet? That's the kind of person Father is. What kind of person throws up her hands and describes this fish as "awful stuff"? That is the kind of person Aunt Louisa is. Now, answer the following questions.

4. Which word **best** describes Father?
   - A. Rude
   - B. Serious
   - C. Enthusiastic
   - D. Understanding

5. Which word **best** describes Aunt Louisa?
   - A. Angry
   - B. Honest
   - C. Frivolous
   - D. Disapproving

**Identify the conflict.**

Most plots in fiction develop out of conflict. The main character in a story might be in conflict with another person, society, nature, or himself or herself. He or she may have to overcome a basic problem, such as a fear of flying or a lost pet. The plot of a story will develop and eventually resolve these conflicts.

6. So far, what is the basic conflict of "Slom Season"?
   - A. Father loves slom, but Aunt Louisa hates it.
   - B. Not enough slom is available to go around.
   - C. The slom has taken too long to come into season.
   - D. During the winter, Father has to eat dried or pickled fish.

If Father and Aunt Louisa become the main characters of the developing story—and they do—then the conflict must focus on both of them—and it does. The children are the "third party" observers of the conflict. For now, they are on Father's side.

# *Slom Season*

## (Continued)

. . . It was always a great disappointment to us girls that Aunt Louisa did not share our delight. Still, she must have had some appreciation of the event, for she said something in a low tone to the housekeeper, who smiled and nodded approval. Whereupon we were told not to let our father know the slom had come; it was to be a surprise for his supper.

We watched with fascination as the housekeeper prepared the fish, deheading them and gutting them, but leaving on the tail. Then she would wash them, dip them in flour, and place them gently in the frying pan. There the fish sizzled and sputtered until they were done to a crisp, brown perfection.

We would file into the dining room biting our lips to keep from smiling. When Father spotted the fish on the table, his face lit up, and he would say, "At last we have some real food in this house!" And we, after keeping the secret so well, would burst into peals of laughter.

Even Aunt Louisa would admit the slom was not too terrible.

The next day the fisherman would return with a whole pound of slom. Father came to the kitchen to pay him in person, and requested that he continue to bring us fish. "For heaven's sake, don't take them to anyone else." And we would enjoy another feast like we had the day before.

The third day, the fishermen delivered enough slom to fill a small bucket. Slom was now served at the family table both for breakfast as well as supper. The housekeeper complained of the quantities of butter the fish were taking. The butter tub had been full only a few days before, and she could already see the bottom. That was the beginning of the end.

More slom came the next day, and at dinner, Father made a fuss when he was served canned ham. "I don't see why I should eat this canned food when the pantry is full of nice, fresh fish." So from then on, it was slom by morning, noon, and night. Soon all but Father began to sicken of slom. We couldn't help but sigh as we saw the everlasting slom set before us at the table, and we took smaller portions at each meal.

But Father kept on buying. And, true to his word, the fisherman who brought the first slom came faithfully every day, and sometimes twice a day. Once happy to escape the routine, the housekeepers now longed to get back to their regular household chores. If Father wasn't home, they would shoo the fisherman away when he arrived with his bucket of slom. It went on like that for weeks.

*(To be continued . . .)*

## Look for important contrasts and comparisons.

Now we have a fuller sense of the conflict between Aunt Louisa and Father. At first, Father seemed "enthusiastic"; now we might add "demanding" and "unreasonable." In contrast, Louisa, instead of being seen as the "party-pooper," is now the children's strongest ally. Her initial "disapproval" is seen in a new light.

7. How are Aunt Louisa and Father different?
    A. Aunt Louisa is sensible; Father is not.
    B. Father is liked by the children; Aunt Louisa is not.
    C. Aunt Louisa is fond of slom; Father only tolerates it.
    D. Aunt Louisa is liked by the housekeeper; Father is not.

## Pay attention to narrative "clues."

8. The author mentions Aunt Louisa's "appreciation" of the first slom of the season in order to show that —
    A. she can never tell what Aunt Louisa will do
    B. Aunt Louisa is not sure whether she likes slom
    C. Aunt Louisa was just pretending to dislike slom
    D. Aunt Louisa is being a good sport about the slom

Details such as Aunt Louisa's playing along with the girls add to the depth of her character.

## *Slom Season*

### (Continued)

. . . At last, Aunt Louisa declared an end to our suffering. That afternoon, the housekeeper prepared boiled slom for dinner. Now, one look at boiled slom lying pale and corpse-like on your plate, and even the most die-hard of appetites goes dull. We all watched as Father lifted his fork to his mouth.

"What in heaven's name is this?" he asked.

"We're all out of butter, and since you will have nothing but slom, we had no choice but to boil it," said Louisa. "If you ask me," she added, "I think it tastes no worse that way than any other."

Father made no reply, but there was a moment of uncertainty for us. Would Father put down his fork and dash off to the pantry, only to find our stock of butter? What would he say to us then? Fortunately, he did nothing of the kind.

After that dinner, Father bought no more slom. "What was the use," he grumbled, "when the housekeepers are too lazy to fix it properly?" No one contradicted him, though we all knew that he was just as glad as we were to see the last of the slom.

**Identify the overall mood the author creates.**

The mood is based on setting, word choice, the characters, the plot, and almost everything else in a story. How do we feel when the story is finished? If the housekeeper had quit, we'd feel a little sour. If Father had been a bad sport, we'd conclude that he really was a pain. Instead, Father stays "in character," even while his human side is revealed: He too gets sick of slom.

9. The mood of this selection is —
   A. Grim
   B. Playful
   C. Idealistic
   D. Moralistic

 **Understand the difference between biography and autobiography.**

Stories about the lives of real people are not "made-up" fiction, but they are important narrative forms since they are about "something happening to someone, somewhere." Biography and autobiography are halfway between fiction and "informational texts," depending on how they are told. Lagerlöf's piece, with its skillful structuring of plot, is certainly closer to fiction than it is to mere information.

**Biography:** The subject of the biography is the main character, and his or her life is the plot.

**Autobiography:** This is the story of a person's life told by himself or herself. You will recognize autobiography by the use of the first-person pronoun, "I."

10. This selection is written in the form of —
    A. biography
    B. autobiography
    C. historical fiction
    D. action adventure

## Summing Up

As you answer questions about story elements, keep in mind the following tips:

• Understand the different narrative genres.

• Understand the "building blocks" of storytelling.

• Understand plot development.

• Get to know the characters through what they say and do.

• Identify the conflict.

• Look for important contrasts and comparisons.

• Pay attention to narrative clues.

• Identify the overall mood the author creates.

• Understand the difference between biography and autobiography.

## PRACTICE SELECTION

**Directions:** Read the selection and answer the questions that follow.

from

## *Starship to Sirius*

by Reggie Blackpool

Toby sat slumped in a chair in the ship's main hall, staring at the huge viewscreen. Sirius was a small blue disk against the perfect blackness of space. Toby remembered when it had simply been a tiny dot among thousands of other stars. Then it had grown into a sharp, distinct point of blue light. Now it was so close, Toby felt he could almost reach out and touch it. The problem was, he didn't know if he wanted to.

He knew he should be excited. This was the moment everyone on the ship had waited for their whole lives. Actually, it had been even longer than that. The *Pegasus* had left Earth 150 years earlier, bound for Danae, a small, Earth-like planet in orbit around Sirius. *Pegasus* was one of the "generational starships" that had been sent from Earth to establish colonies on <u>habitable</u> planets relatively nearby.

The key word, though, was "relatively." Even though Sirius was close to the Sun in astronomical terms, it still took much longer than a human lifetime to travel there. Each generational starship was as big as a small city, and the passengers who left on it knew they would never see their final destination. That dream would only come true for their descendants.

Toby's great-great-grandparents had been among those first passengers. How brave they must have been, Toby often thought. He doubted he had that sort of courage in him. What made him feel even worse was that he wasn't even grateful to be one of those who would actually land on Danae. He was 15 years old. He and his friends would be the first generation to live their entire adult lives on the new planet. But as he stared at the blue disk on the screen, Toby wished the ship would just go right by Danae.

The touch of a hand on his shoulder startled him.

"Toby?" It was his mom. "I thought I'd find you here."

She sat down next to him and gently squeezed his arm, her face practically glowing. "I can't believe it's only going to be a few more weeks, can you? The whole ship's buzzing. It's amazing."

"Yeah, I guess," was all Toby could say in reply.

"What's wrong, Toby?" his mom asked. "Are you thinking about Grandpa?"

*I'm like an open book to Mom*, Toby thought. He nodded and said, "I just can't stop wishing he was here."

"I know, Toby. He's been on your mind a lot lately, hasn't he?"

He had. It was over a year since he had died, but now that their destination was finally within reach, Toby found himself thinking about his grandfather almost daily. He had always planned on exploring the wonders of their new home with Grandpa. Toby remembered Grandpa explaining something called "fishing."

"My grandfather, the one who left Earth on the *Pegasus*, told me all about it," Grandpa had said. "He told me it was something that grandfathers did with their grandkids on Earth. Of course, I never had a chance to do it with him. You need lakes and streams to fish, and even the *Pegasus* doesn't have those. But he made me promise that when I reached Danae and had grandkids of my own, I'd take them fishing and see what we could catch on the new planet. He told me the water on Earth was blue. I wonder, what color will it be on Danae? Well, I guess we'll find out when we get there."

*Now that won't happen*, Toby thought.

"We all miss him, Toby," his mother said, "but more than anybody, Grandpa would want you to be thrilled about finally getting here."

*He sure would*, Toby thought. But without Grandpa, leaving the *Pegasus*— the only home he had ever known—made Toby nervous.

A bright streak of light appeared on the viewscreen, headed for the star. It was one of the high-speed probes regularly sent out from the ship to gather data on Danae before the *Pegasus* arrived. In only a few weeks, they'd be there to see the planet for themselves.

"I've been looking forward to this since before I can remember, Mom," Toby said. "But now, without Grandpa, it just won't be the same." Deep down, he was still excited by the adventure waiting for him. He was looking forward to the challenges ahead. *But without Grandpa*, Toby wondered, *how am I going to do in this new world?*

# Sample Story Elements Questions

**Directions:** Read each question and circle the letter of the correct answer.

1. In this selection, Toby experiences conflict with —
   A. himself
   B. his mother
   C. his grandfather
   D. the captain of the *Pegasus*

2. Which word **best** describes how Toby's mother feels about arriving at Danae?
   A. Unhappy
   B. Excited
   C. Terrified
   D. Interested

3. The rest of *Starship to Sirius* will **most likely** center around which of the following conflicts?
   A. Toby's search for confidence in his new home
   B. The colonists' fight to survive on a remote planet
   C. Toby's efforts to reel in a huge fish on the Pegasus
   D. Toby's struggle to get his mother to understand him

4. In this selection, the overall mood is that of —
   A. joy
   B. fear
   C. concern
   D. happiness

5. This selection is written in the form of —
   A. a folk tale
   B. a biography
   C. science fiction
   D. historical fiction

# Additional Practice Questions

**Directions:** Now answer some other types of questions about the reading selection. You can learn about these question types in other lessons of this book.

6.  How long has Toby lived on the *Pegasus?*
    A. His whole life
    B. Several weeks
    C. A little over a year
    D. Since his grandfather died

7.  Which of the following events actually happens **first**?
    A. Grandpa tells Toby about fishing.
    B. The *Pegasus* leaves Earth for Danae.
    C. Toby's mother finds him in the main hall.
    D. Toby remembers when Sirius was only a tiny dot.

8.  Why had Grandpa talked to Toby about going fishing on Danae together?
    A. His favorite grandfather had gone fishing with him.
    B. His father had shared memories of fishing with him.
    C. Toby was just at the age that he had been when he first went fishing.
    D. His grandfather said it was something grandfathers did with their grandkids.

9.  In this selection, the word *habitable* means —
    A. cozy
    B. nearby
    C. livable
    D. understandable

10. Of the following characters, who was probably the **last** to have gone fishing on Earth?
    A. Toby's father
    B. Toby's grandfather
    C. Toby's great grandfather
    D. Toby's great-great grandfather

# Lesson 9: Poetry Elements

**Figurative language** is language that goes beyond the literal way of saying something. For example, if a friend says, "I'm so hungry I could eat a horse," we know that what he really wants is large quantities of chow, not an actual horse. He's speaking figuratively. If he were speaking literally, well, *that* would be a little scary.

Figurative language appears frequently in everyday speech. A sudden realization may "hit you like a ton of bricks." You might "strike out" on a pop quiz, find yourself faced with "mountains" of homework, or claim that your P.E. class is a "nightmare."

Writers often aim for fresh, original comparisons using figures of speech. Similes, metaphors, and personification "activate" the reader's mind with vivid comparisons, adding interest to any kind of text.

**Learn the four basic types of figurative language.**

In every English class from now on, you will probably be asked to learn the difference between similes and metaphors. It's easy to do, so why not start here?

A **simile** uses *like* or *as* to compare two things.

A **metaphor** makes a comparison by saying one thing *is* another or by implying such through a careful choice of words.

Here are two more types of figurative language.

**Personification** is the use of human qualities to describe animals, objects, or ideas.

**Hyperbole** is a deliberate use of exaggeration in order to get a laugh, make a point, or persuade.

**Directions:** Read the following selection and answer questions 1 through 4.

adapted from

## *The Mysterious Island*

by Jules Verne

  After being suspended for an instant aloft, the balloon began to descend again, gas escaping from the large tear in its fabric. The five men had done all that men could do. No human efforts could save them now. At four o'clock they were only five hundred feet above the surface of the water.
  The balloon, which the wind had driven southwest since daybreak, was still nearly thirty miles from the tiny island. The voyagers could distinctly see

that solid spot which they must reach at any cost, whether inhabited or desolate, whether hospitable or not.

It was evident that the balloon could no longer support itself. Several times already the crests of enormous waves had licked the bottom of the net, making it still heavier. The balloon only half rose, like a bird with a wounded wing. It plunged into the sea again and the travelers were beaten by the furious waters. The balloon case bulged once more, and the wind, taking it, drove it along like a ship. Suddenly, after having been struck by a tremendous sea, it made an unexpected bound, met a current of wind, and mounted to a height of fifteen hundred feet.

1. Read the following sentence from the selection:

    Several times already the crests of enormous waves had licked the bottom of the net, making it still heavier.

    What type of figurative language is being used in this sentence?
    A. Simile
    B. Metaphor
    C. Hyperbole
    D. Personification

2. How do you know?

    _____

    _____

    _____

3. Read the following sentence from the selection:

    The balloon only half rose, like a bird with a wounded wing.

    What type of figurative language is being used in this sentence?
    A. Simile
    B. Metaphor
    C. Hyperbole
    D. Personification

4. How do you know?

    _____

    _____

    _____

**Use your imagination to picture *both* things being compared in a simile or metaphor.**

Read the following question.

5. When the author compares the balloon to a wounded bird, he means that —
   A. it has a leak
   B. it is getting frenzied
   C. it is crying out in pain
   D. it cannot fly very well

Neither a wounded bird nor a leaking hot air balloon can fly very well, and the description that follows the simile in the text shows that to be true.

Let's try two more questions.

6. When the author describes the waters as "furious," he means that they are —
   A. slightly choppy
   B. rough and wavy
   C. still and smooth
   D. flowing quickly

7. Read the following sentence from the selection.

   The balloon case bulged once more, and the wind, taking it, drove it along like a ship.

   In this sentence, the author means that —
   A. the balloon moved in the direction of a nearby ship
   B. the balloon was filling with wind and slowly floating higher
   C. the balloon's case contained controls similar to those found on a ship
   D. the balloon's direction and movement was controlled by the wind

**Don't be afraid of poetry. Relax and "experience" the images.**

The state test may contain a selection or two of poetry. To do your best on this part of the test, relax as you read. Allow yourself to experience the images the poem presents.

**Directions:** Read the selection below. It will be used to explain the tips that follow.

# A Patch of Old Snow

## by Robert Frost

There's a patch of old snow in a corner,
  That I should have guessed
Was a blow-away paper the rain
  Had brought to a rest.

It is speckled with grime as if
  Small print overspread it,
The news of a day I've forgotten—
  If I ever read it.

> **Robert Frost** (1874–1963) spent most of his life in New England. His poems derive their sometimes gruff, common-sense insights from his observations of the natural world. Frost also wrote "Stopping by Woods on a Snowy Evening," "After Apple Picking," and "The Road Less Traveled."

**Understand the difference between realistic and figurative description.**

8. In this selection, a patch of snow is compared to —
    A. grime
    B. a corner
    C. a newspaper
    D. a speckled pigeon

The words *grime, corner,* and *speckled* all appear in the poem, but don't let that fool you. *Grime* (A) and *corner* (B) are realistic parts of the description. Had the author compared the snow to "a speckled pigeon" (D), that would have been figurative language. But no birds are mentioned in the poem.

What about *newspaper* (C)?

**"Add up" the evidence to develop the picture.**

The word *newspaper* is not in the text. But read these lines from the first stanza: "There's a patch of old snow . . ./That I should have guessed/Was a blow-away paper . . .". What is a "blow-away paper?" you might ask. It could be a bakery bag, a receipt, a love letter, anything. This is actually how the poet gets our attention.

The second stanza mentions "small print," an image that perhaps calls a newspaper to mind. The last two lines tell us that the paper contains "news . . ./If I ever read it."

**Identify what the two things being compared have in common.**

9. In the box on the next page, list ways in which a patch of old snow and the newspaper described in the poem are **alike**.

**Directions:** Read the selection below. It will be used to explain the tip that follows.

## *Post-War Famine*

by Minerva Plunkett

In the years after World War II (1939–1945), developing countries such as Mexico, India, and China, lived in the shadow of famine, or food shortage resulting in widespread hunger. Their rapidly expanding populations had simply hit the wall of their ability to produce food in traditional ways. A bad year for crops spelled death and suffering for millions. The United States gave away a lot of its extra grain to these countries, but such short-term help did not solve the basic famine problem.

 **To figure out the meaning of an unknown expression, substitute the answer choices for it.**

If you don't know the meaning of a figurative expression, try plugging in the answer choices in its place. Try this on the following question.

10. In the first sentence, the phrase "in the shadow" means —
    A. in suspicion
    B. with the threat
    C. under the protection
    D. in complete ignorance

Choice A: . . . developing countries . . . lived *in suspicion* of famine. . . .

Choice B: . . . developing countries . . . lived *with the threat* of famine. . . .

Choice C: . . . developing countries . . . lived *under the protection* of famine. . . .

Choice D: . . . developing countries . . . lived *in complete ignorance* of famine. . . .

Which choice makes the most sense in the context of the selection?

**Answering some figurative language questions may require a mix of strategies.**

Read the following question.

11. In this selection, the phrase "hit the wall" means —
   A. reached the limit
   B. became exhausted
   C. approached the end
   D. experienced a conflict

First, use the substitution strategy to eliminate some answer choices. To say that expanding populations "experienced a conflict" (D) with their ability to produce is somewhat mild, given the circumstances reported. "Became exhausted" (B) makes even less sense when substituted.

The question is whether the countries approached the end (C) or reached the limit (A). Both sound reasonable enough. Here is where you return to the figure itself. Picture yourself riding a "scooter" into a wall, at high speed (the excerpt says "rapidly"). Now, have you "reached" this wall (or limit), or have you just "approached" it? Your imaginary scrapes and bruises should give you a clue.

## Summing Up

As you answer questions about figurative language, keep in mind the following tips:

- Learn the four basic types of figurative language.
- Use your imagination to picture *both* things being compared in a simile or metaphor.
- Don't be afraid of poetry. Relax and experience the images.
- Understand the difference between realistic and figurative description.
- Add up the evidence to develop the picture.
- Identify what the two things in a simile or metaphor have in common.
- To figure out the meaning of an unknown expression, substitute the answer choices for it.
- Answering some figurative language questions may require a mix of strategies.

### PRACTICE SELECTION

**Directions:** Read the selection and answer the questions that follow.

## *Runaway Train*

by Minerva Plunkett

My name is Harriet Tubman,
and I'm a train conductor.
My train makes lots of connections,
but the only destination
I know of is freedom.

My train is a runaway train,
Its "passengers" once slaves;
My train is a runaway train,
Never gonna be stopped.
Yes, my train is a runaway train,
but I never run my train off the track,
and I never lost a passenger.

My train is invisible;
That's why they call it "underground."
My train doesn't run on coal,
It runs on the kindness of strangers.
You don't need a ticket to get on board,
But don't forget your password.

**Harriet Tubman** (1820–1913) was an African American who was called the "Moses of her people." She helped more than 300 slaves escape before the Civil War. Tubman and others like her led escaped slaves from the South to the North with the help of a secret network of people that came to be known as the **Underground Railroad**.

# Sample Poetry Elements Questions

**Directions:** Read each question and circle the letter of the correct answer.

1. What is the train mentioned in the poem?
   A. An actual train that Tubman worked on as a conductor
   B. A railroad system used by slave owners to transport slaves
   C. Tubman's method of bringing escaped slaves to the North
   D. A secret network that brought supplies such as coal to the North

2. The idea of a train is used in the poem as —
   A. a simile
   B. a metaphor
   C. an hyperbole
   D. personification

3. Who are the passengers on the train?
   A. Strangers
   B. Slave owners
   C. Escaped slaves
   D. Train conductors

4. What does the author mean by calling the train "invisible"?
   A. The train is kept a secret.
   B. The train comes only at night.
   C. The train runs under the ground.
   D. The train can be heard but not seen.

5. What do the following lines mean?
   > My train doesn't run on coal,
   > It runs on the kindness of strangers.

   A. Strangers can board the train only by using a password.
   B. Strangers work together to help runaway slaves escape to freedom.
   C. Strangers offer free railway tickets to slaves who want to travel North.
   D. Strangers offer free coal to the conductors to keep the train running.

# Additional Practice Questions

**Directions:** Now answer some other types of questions about the selection. You can learn about these question types in other lessons of this book.

6. Why is it necessary that the train be "invisible"?

_____

_____

_____

_____

_____

7. What is the poem **mainly** about?
   A. A train that never stops running
   B. A woman who dreams about conducting a train
   C. A slave who tries to escape with the help of strangers
   D. A woman's determination to free others from slavery

# unit 4

# Written Response Skills

The New York English Language Arts Test isn't just about reading. Portions of the exam will test your writing and listening skills as well.

In this unit, you will practice composing responses to passages you read yourself or hear read aloud to you. You will learn what qualities your writing will need in order for you to earn your highest possible score. You also will review several grammar, punctuation, and spelling rules—a few more tools to help you do your best.

# Lesson 10: Planning and Composing

Imagine you have just read or listened to a selection. Now you are asked to write something brilliant about it—in two pages or less. You might wish you had a few days to think about it, but you don't. If only you could do a little research on the Internet, form a discussion group, talk to your mom—but you can't. You are on your own, and the clock is ticking. How do you begin?

Open-ended test questions have a way of putting you "on the spot." In this lesson, you will practice tackling this question type. The key? Breaking the task into manageable parts. Here are a few tips to help you do just that.

**Carefully read or listen to the entire selection.**

On the state test, each response question will be connected to a selection in some way. Be sure to read or listen carefully to the entire selection before attempting this question type.

**If the selection is read aloud to you, listen for important information.**

For one portion of the test, you will listen to a selection read aloud. The first time the selection is read, listen carefully but do not take notes. As the selection is being read, ask yourself general questions such as the following:

- **What kind of selection is it?** Does it tell a fictional story? Is it a poem? Or is it a factual article about real persons, places, events, or ideas?
- **What is the main idea?** What is the selection mostly about?

The second time the selection is read, take a few notes. Here are some things you might want to remember:

- **If the selection is fiction,** who are the main characters? What problem do the characters face? What are the main events? How is the problem solved?
- **If the selection is nonfiction,** what is the main idea? What are the important details that support the main idea?

Perhaps you're thinking, "Hey, I'll just frantically write down everything I hear." Bad idea. It is more important to understand the main idea and to remember a few important details. If you get too caught up in writing down every detail, you will miss the "big picture" the author is trying to get across.

**Read the question carefully.**

Written response questions can be worded in many different ways. Some will have more than one part. Be sure to read each question carefully and answer it thoroughly.

**Plan your writing.**

The state test will give you space to plan your writing. Take advantage of this. There are many ways to plan and organize your writing. Here are just a few:

- **Brainstorming** is writing down any idea that pops into your head, no matter how strange or stupid it might seem at the time. (Don't worry: The work you do on your "Planning Page" will not be scored.)

  Imagine you were asked to tell who your favorite movie or television character of all time is, then explain why that person is your favorite. Your brainstorming might look something like this.

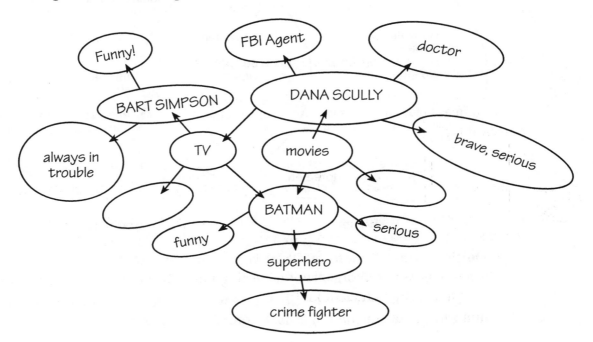

- **Freewriting** is another simple way to generate ideas. When you freewrite, you pick a topic and write nonstop as fast as you can. A minute or two usually will be enough time to generate a lot of ideas. You don't have to worry about spelling, grammar, or punctuation. The most important thing about freewriting is to *keep writing.*

  Imagine you are asked to write about what you think is the biggest problem in your school. Your freewriting might look something like this:

  *Lunch is a problem, the lines are too long and we barely have time to eat then all you can do is bring your lunch and what else? there aren't enough computers and that's my favorite thing but I don't get a chance to use them much so more money for computers would be nice but maybe the problems money*

- **Graphic organizers** can help you organize your ideas visually. You can use a graphic organizer to group your ideas and show how they are related.

  Imagine you are asked to write an essay comparing electronic mail (e-mail) to mail delivered the traditional way, by the U.S. Postal Service. Your ideas might be organized like this:

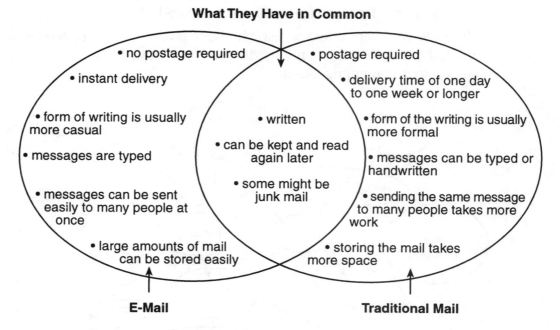

**What They Have in Common**

E-Mail side:
- no postage required
- instant delivery
- form of writing is usually more casual
- messages are typed
- messages can be sent easily to many people at once
- large amounts of mail can be stored easily

Common (center):
- written
- can be kept and read again later
- some might be junk mail

Traditional Mail side:
- postage required
- delivery time of one day to one week or longer
- form of the writing is usually more formal
- messages can be typed or handwritten
- sending the same message to many people takes more work
- storing the mail takes more space

**E-Mail**          **Traditional Mail**

- **Outlines** are a more formal way to organize your writing. Your outline should show how you will organize the writing into a beginning, a middle, and an end.

  Imagine you are asked to write an essay telling your opinion about school uniforms. Your outline might look something like this:

  I. Introduction: I think school uniforms are a great idea.

  II. Ideas supporting my opinion
  
   A. Students and families would spend less money on school clothes.
   
   B. Students wouldn't have to think about what to wear to school each day.
   
   C. Students wouldn't try to "out-dress" each other.

  III. Conclusion: Our school should adopt a policy requiring students to wear uniforms. The people who would benefit most are the students.

**Support your answer with ideas from the selection.**

Most written response questions will ask you to link your ideas to those found in the selection. Some will ask you to connect ideas from more than one selection. Be sure to follow the instructions closely and to support your writing with ideas from the selection.

## PRACTICE ACTIVITY 1

**Directions:** For this activity, you will listen to a poem titled "A Night with a Wolf." Then you will answer questions about what you have heard.

The poem will be read twice. The first time it is read, listen carefully but do not take notes. As it is read the second time, use the space below to take notes. You may use these notes to answer the questions that follow.

# *Notes*

# *Planning Page*

You may use this page to plan your answer to Number 1. Do not write your final answer on this page. Your writing on this page will NOT be scored. Write your answer on the next page.

**Directions:** Answer the following question. You may use the notes you wrote on page 102 to help you write your response. Use a pencil for this exercise; it will be easier to make changes in your work later.

1. Discuss the speaker's view toward wolves based on his experience as described in the poem. In your discussion, be sure to include the following:
   - descriptions of the speaker's experience
   - how the speaker was affected by his experience

Check your writing for correct spelling, grammar, and punctuation.

_____

_____

_____

_____

_____

_____

_____

_____

_____

_____

_____

_____

_____

_____

### Check your writing.

Your writing will not be scored based on your personal opinions. It will be scored on such things as organization, clarity, grammar, spelling, and so on. The following checklist tells a few things you should think about as you plan, compose, edit, and revise your writing.

## You will earn your best score if:

❑ Your writing is well organized, with a beginning, a middle, and an end.

❑ Your writing stays focused on the topic.

❑ Your ideas are clearly expressed.

❑ You answer the question accurately and completely.

❑ You connect your own ideas to the ideas in the selection.

❑ You support your ideas with examples.

❑ Your writing is interesting and enjoyable to read.

❑ You use correct grammar, spelling, punctuation, and paragraphing.

❑ Your handwriting is easy for others to read.

## PRACTICE ACTIVITY 2

**Directions**: Complete each of the following activities using the writing you did for Practice Activity 1.

2. Use the checklist above to review the writing you did for Practice Activity 1 (page 103). You may make any changes you wish directly on the page.

3. Trade your writing with a classmate. Use the checklist to evaluate your classmate's writing. Then meet to discuss each other's work. Be sure to tell your classmate what you like best about his or her writing, along with a few suggestions for improving the writing.

## Summing Up

As you compose your answers to written response questions, keep in mind the following tips:

- Carefully read or listen to the entire selection.
- If the selection is read aloud to you, listen for important information.
- Read the question carefully.
- Plan your writing.
- Support your answer with ideas from the selection.
- Check your writing.

## PRACTICE SELECTION

**Directions:** Read the selection and answer the questions that follow.

# Will the Wolf Survive?

by Arthur Figgis

Established in 1872, Yellowstone was America's first national park. The park is mostly in the northwest corner of Wyoming, with some land in Montana and Idaho. Yellowstone's spectacular scenery makes it one of the most-visited parks in the national park system. It's the natural habitat of many wild animals, including the grizzly and black bear, bison, antelope, and bighorn sheep.

The wolf, too, is native to Yellowstone. For much of the 20th century, however, wolves were rare in the park. Starting around 1910, the United States government encouraged wolf hunting in and near the park. The idea was to cut down on the number of predator animals in the area. The effect was to almost wipe out the wolf population.

Today, the wolf is making a comeback. For years, the National Park Service and conservation groups hoped to somehow restore the endangered wolf population. Finally, in 1995, a formal wolf recovery program began. Now, about 125 wolves live in different packs around the park. The wolves are very shy and stay away from humans; sometimes, however, lucky visitors may see one or more. Even if a visitor doesn't see the wolves, he or she might hear the eerie, mournful howling as a dominant wolf calls its pack together.

Not everyone is glad to see the wolves return. Some people fear that wolves will attack humans visiting the park. Wolves tend to shy away from humans, however. In fact, there have been no reports of wild wolves attacking humans in the lower 48 states. Mountain lions, bears, and bison cause more injuries in America's national parks than wolves do.

Wolves have killed some livestock belonging to ranchers around the park. (In those cases, pro-wolf organizations have paid the ranchers fair market value for their lost livestock.) Some hunters also oppose the wolf recovery program. That's because wolves kill big-game animals such as elk, mule deer, and moose.

**Ranges of the Yellowstone Wolf Packs**

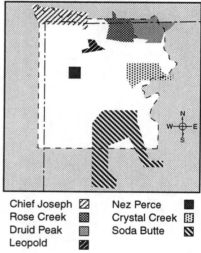

Chief Joseph ▨   Nez Perce ■
Rose Creek ▩   Crystal Creek ▦
Druid Peak ▨   Soda Butte ◺
Leopold ▨

*Each pack of Yellowstone wolves was named after the area in which it was originally released. This map shows the "ranges," or roaming areas, of several of the packs, based on data gathered in 1998.*

In 1997, ruling in favor of ranchers and hunters, a Wyoming judge declared that the wolf recovery program should stop. The case quickly moved to federal appeals court, where it has yet to be decided. The wolf recovery program is a heated issue in the Yellowstone region. No matter what the appeals court decides, emotions will continue to run high between people who favor the wolf program and those who oppose it. Unfortunately, it is the wolves that are caught in the middle.

| Wolf Pack | Adult Wolves | | Young Wolves | |
|---|---|---|---|---|
| | 8/97 | 5/98 | 8/97 | 5/98 |
| Chief Joseph | 2 | 3 | 10 | 6 |
| Crystal Creek | 2 | 5 | 2 | 3 |
| Druid Peak | 2 | 2 | 0 | 4 |
| Leopold | 5 | 4 | 5 | 5 |
| Nez Perce | 4 | 2 | 3 | 4 |
| Rose Creek | 7 | 5 | 15 | 9 |
| Soda Butte | 4 | 4 | 3 | 4 |

# Sample Questions

**Directions:** Read each question and answer it in the space provided.

1. In the graphic organizer below, compare the ideas of those who support the wolf recovery program with those who are against it.

**The Wolf Recovery Program**

| Ideas Supporting the Program | Ideas Against the Program |
| --- | --- |
| | |

2. What is the **most likely** reason the author wrote this article? Use ideas from the article to support your answer.

_____

_____

_____

_____

_____

_____

# *Planning Page*

You may use this page to plan your answer to Number 3. Do not write your final answer on this page. Your writing on this page will NOT be scored. Write your answer on the next page.

**Directions:** Answer the following question. You may use the notes you wrote on page 109 to help you write your response. Use a pencil for this exercise; it will be easier to make changes in your work later.

3. Do you think it is a good idea to release wolves in an area such as Yellowstone National Park? Why or why not? You may use ideas from both the article "Will the Wolf Survive?" and the poem "A Night with a Wolf" in your answer.

_____

_____

_____

_____

_____

_____

_____

_____

_____

_____

_____

_____

_____

_____

_____

# Additional Practice Questions

**Directions:** Now answer some other types of questions about the reading selection. You can learn more about these question types in other lessons of this book.

4. Which wolf pack is **most likely** to threaten livestock belonging to ranches outside the park?
   A. Leopold
   B. Soda Butte
   C. Nez Perce
   D. Crystal Creek

5. Which wolf pack has the smallest roaming area?
   A. Nez Perce
   B. Soda Butte
   C. Chief Joseph
   D. Crystal Creek

6. Which wolf pack is the largest in Yellowstone as of May 1998?
   A. Leopold
   B. Rose Creek
   C. Chief Joseph
   D. Crystal Creek

7. Which wolf pack showed a drop in the number of adults between August of 1997 and May of 1998?
   A. Leopold
   B. Soda Butte
   C. Druid Peak
   D. Chief Joseph

8. How many packs saw an increase in the number of young wolves between August of 1997 and May of 1998?
   A. 2
   B. 3
   C. 4
   D. 5

9. If the largest wolf pack in the park roamed outside Yellowstone, it is **most likely** that the number of complaints by ranchers would —
   A. increase
   B. decrease
   C. remain the same
   D. can't tell from the information given

# Lesson 11: Sentences

*The old pirate slipped a creased and dirty sheet of parchment into his cabin boy's pocket just before he was forced to walk the plank. "A treasure you'll find," he whispered to the boy. "The clues for a rich man are contained. Good-bye, Miles. The hungry sharks a dinner awaits."*

*Unfortunately, the pirate wrote about as clearly as he spoke, "Green Parrot Cove the place. At first light, go straight. Along the shadow of the last palm. Twenty paces, then turn. Six more. Deeply dig."*

*What did it all mean? Fortunately, Miles had been the pirate's cabin boy long enough to understand him. "Clear it is," he said. "And perfectly, so a wealthy man I'll make of me."*

Do you speak in proper, grammatical sentences? Most of us do in formal conversations; however, most of us probably don't when we're talking casually with our family or friends. The same is true of reading and writing.

Most written material would be out of control if the writer constantly threw in fragments or run-on sentences. And casual conversations would soon become stuffy if we had to observe proper sentence construction all the time. Yet, some organization is necessary for our thoughts to make sense.

This lesson will review sentence fragments and run-on sentences, two major flaws in formal writing. Let's start by taking a little test.

**Directions:** Read the following sentences. Underline the sentence that best presents the idea.

*Cola and coffee contain caffeine they make me jittery.*

*Cola and coffee, containing caffeine and making me jittery.*

*Cola and coffee contain caffeine; they make me jittery.*

Which did you choose? The third example is the only one that is grammatically correct. What exactly is wrong with the other two? Read on . . .

© 1999 Buckle Down Publishing Company. DO NOT DUPLICATE.

# On and On and On

The first sentence below is an example of a **run-on sentence**. In this case, the run-on sentence has two sets of subjects, as well as two verbs. The writer has strung together two complete thoughts without separating them.

> **Wrong**    *Cola and coffee contain caffeine they make me jittery.*

1. What are the subjects in the example sentence above?
   (Hint: One of them is a compound subject.)

   _____

   _____

2. What are the verbs in the example sentence above?

   _____

   _____

Once you recognize run-ons, fixing them is a fairly simple process.

 **One way to fix a run-on sentence is to split it into two (or more) new sentences. To do this, place a period at the end of each complete thought.**

> **Wrong**    *Chumbawamba and Weezer are my favorite groups I like their music no matter what kind of mood I'm in.*

> **OK**    *Chumbawamba and Weezer are my favorite groups. I like their music no matter what kind of mood I'm in.*

Some run-on sentences are the result of a "comma fault." This generally means the writer recognizes that there are multiple thoughts in the sentence. He or she uses a comma to separate them, rather than end punctuation or a semicolon. For example:

> **Wrong**    *Chumbawamba and Weezer are my favorite groups, I like their music no matter what kind of mood I'm in.*

The cure is the same: Place a period at the end of the first complete thought.

> **OK**    *Chumbawamba and Weezer are my favorite groups. I like their music no matter what kind of mood I'm in.*

**Another way to fix a run-on sentence is to join two complete thoughts with a connecting word (such as and, but, or, nor, while, which, because, etc.).**

OK       *Because Chumbawamba and Weezer are my favorite groups, I like their music no matter what kind of mood I'm in.*

or

OK       *Chumbawamba and Weezer are my favorite groups, which means I like their music no matter what kind of mood I'm in.*

Notice in the examples above that the sentences now contain **dependent clauses** they didn't contain before. (A dependent clause is an incomplete sentence.) Both examples require commas to set off the clauses.

3. Underline the dependent clause in each example sentence above.

## All Broken Up

The second sentence of the opening examples is a **sentence fragment**. A fragment is a piece of something, not a whole thing in itself. Likewise, a sentence fragment is not a whole sentence. It is missing either the subject, the verb, or, sometimes, both the subject and the verb.

**Every sentence must have a subject and a verb. If a fragment is missing a verb, add one.**

*Kit Kat bars and Hershey's Kisses, containing chocolate and making me drool.*

The fragment has a compound subject, *Kit Kat bars and Hershey's Kisses*. This subject has two participles attached to it: *containing* and *making*. Participles are verb forms used to describe something rather than to show action.

4. Rewrite the sentence fragment so that it makes sense.

_____

_____

**If a fragment is missing a subject, add one.**

Read the following sentence fragment.

*Plays steel guitar and keyboard.*

In this case, we don't know *who* does these things; the sentence needs a subject.

5. Make the fragment below into a sentence by adding a subject.

_____ plays steel guitar and keyboard.

**Watch out for fragments that have neither a subject nor a verb.**

*Dancing in the barn, which is a lot of fun unless the cows try to join in.*

Again, *dancing* is a verb form, but not a verb that forms the predicate of a sentence. There is no subject in the fragment. *Which is a lot of fun unless the cows try to join in* does not count as subject or verb, since it is a subordinate clause with no main clause to support it.

## It's All Here

All that's required for a complete sentence are a subject (e.g. *soda*) and a verb (e.g. *fizzes*).

*Soda fizzes.*

Depending on the verb, an object may be necessary, too.

*Licorice contains.*

Contains is a verb that requires an object. Your immediate impulse should be to ask, "Contains what?"

*Licorice contains sugar.*

6. On the line below, write a very brief sentence that contains only a simple subject, a verb, and an object.

_____

## I Thought You Understood

One special case deserves mention here: sentences with an "understood you." When a sentence is a type of a command in which the writer (or speaker) tells someone to do something, the subject (You) is often left out. This is still considered a complete sentence.

> *Please pass the grits.*

The subject is the "understood you." The verb is "pass." We have a complete sentence that just looks like a fragment. This is the same as saying the following:

> *You, pass the grits, please.*

If that sounds a little strange, try saying the sentence with a person's name inserted.

> *Leslie, pass the grits, please.*

7. Now write your own "understood you" sentence on the lines provided.

_____

_____

**PRACTICE ACTIVITY**

**Directions:** In the sentences below, write F in front of each fragment, R in front of each run-on sentence, and C in front of each complete sentence. Then in the space below each group of words, rewrite each fragment or run-on sentence to make a complete sentence or pair of sentences. You may add or take away a few words, as needed.

**Example:** _F_ Whether I believe you once sang at Carnegie Hall.

*I'm not sure whether I believe you once sang at Carnegie Hall.*

___1. The election results, which had, at that point, not been completely tabulated.

___2. To reduce swelling immediately after an injury, apply an ice pack and elevate the injured part.

___3. Boris and Natasha were having another argument, the kind that usually ended with Natasha immobilized in the direct path of an oncoming locomotive.

___4. Completely of its own accord, slithered out of the tub, down to the kitchen, and out of the open door.

___5. The city council came to a decision skateboarders and Roller-Bladers could use the parking ramp, but only after hours.

___6. Nothing better than hot cocoa after shoveling snow from the walk.

___7. The more I try to concentrate, the more my mind keeps wandering.

___8. Yesterday, everything seemed to be in the way of her accomplishing her dreams today those obstacles have all but vanished.

___9. The dogs, exhausted after a long walk through the woods, where they encountered squirrels, rabbits, and a host of intriguing smells.

___10. The envelope, which was addressed to him, had a postmark from Israel.

# Lesson 12: Paragraphs

Paragraphs are the building blocks of writing. Just as a builder requires sound materials to put together a house or a skyscraper, a writer requires sound paragraphs to assemble a story, an essay, or a novel.

In general, paragraphs contain three parts: a **topic sentence**, **supporting sentences**, and a **concluding sentence**. There are exceptions, of course, but you should keep this structure in mind as you prepare for the state test. The following information tells what each part contains.

A topic sentence tells the main idea of a paragraph. Very often, the topic sentence is the first sentence in the paragraph, but it doesn't have to be. Like the main idea of an essay, a topic sentence must be supported with additional information.

The supporting sentences add ideas or facts that reinforce the topic sentence. Each of these supporting sentences contributes in some way to the topic. Sentences that do not build on the topic sentence should be eliminated from the paragraph. They may be moved to another paragraph or deleted altogether.

The concluding sentence sums up the paragraph. It ties the supporting sentences to the topic sentence. The concluding sentence restates the topic sentence but weaves in some of the supporting information.

**Directions:** Read the sample paragraph that follows. Identify the types of sentences contained in the paragraph by writing **T** for topic sentence, **S** for supporting sentences, or **C** for the concluding sentence on the line following each sentence.

> The horn of the spotted unicornfish must have a purpose, but scientists are unsure what that purpose is. _____ Like the legendary beast after which it was named, the unicornfish has a long horn that extends straight out from between its eyes and above its nose. _____ Perhaps the horn is used to frighten the fish's enemies. _____ Perhaps it is used to attract other unicornfish during mating season. _____ Or perhaps the horn's purpose is a mystery, as impossible to solve as the legend of the beast after which it was named. _____

## Types of Paragraphs

The paragraph structure described above is useful in most types of writing, whether it be **narrative**, **descriptive**, **expository**, or **persuasive**. (A notable exception is dialogue.) It's important to understand these types of writing so that you can practice composing the different types of paragraphs before you take the state test.

Narrative writing is storytelling. The story doesn't have to be made up. It may be a factual account of an adventure you lived through, a biographical piece that tells the story of someone's life, or a journal entry describing a specific event that happened to you one day. On the other hand, narrative writing may be a fictional story, a novel, a story poem, or even a play. This kind of writing probably bends the rules of paragraphing more than any other.

Give an example of narrative writing you have read:

_____

Descriptive writing often makes use of the paragraphing rule. It introduces someone or something, then gives details that paint a vivid word picture in the reader's mind. An example of descriptive writing might be a journal that describes what a person has seen while traveling.

Give an example of descriptive writing you have read:

_____

Expository writing introduces an idea and gives facts and/or ideas to explain and clarify it. The paragraphing rule is very useful here. Examples of expository writing may include reports and business letters.

Give an example of expository writing you have read:

_____

Persuasive writing is used to present an idea while attempting to convince readers of its truth. The paragraphing rule is useful because it states, reinforces, and restates the writer's position on a topic. One example of persuasive writing is a newspaper editorial.

Give an example of persuasive writing you have read:

_____

## PRACTICE ACTIVITY

**Directions:** Choose one type of writing (narrative, descriptive, expository, or persuasive). Then write a brief paragraph that includes a topic sentence, at least two supporting sentences, and a concluding sentence. When you have finished, trade work with a partner. Ask him or her to identify what type of writing you have done.

_____

_____

_____

_____

_____

_____

_____

_____

_____

_____

_____

_____

_____

_____

_____

_____

_____

_____

_____

_____

# Lesson 13: Capitalization

*bILL spent an entire tuesDay working on Capitalization at his uncle BOB's repair Shop for Mangled Sentences so he could have a better Chance of getting Into oxford University in engLand.*

By this time in your academic life, people expect you to know the basic rules of capitalization. Even if you're not as bad off as Bill in the example above, it's a good idea to review before you take the test.

The basic rules of capitalization are listed below. Each rule is followed by at least one example. As you read the rules, think of an example of your own. Write your examples on the lines provided.

| Capitalize: | Example: |
|---|---|
| 1. the first letter of the first word of every new sentence | <u>M</u>y cat is cranky. |
| 2. names of cities, counties, states, continents, countries, geographical features | <u>M</u>emphis, <u>T</u>ennessee, <u>A</u>ustralia, <u>B</u>lue <u>R</u>idge <u>M</u>ountains |
| 3. days, months, holidays | <u>M</u>onday, <u>S</u>eptember, <u>L</u>abor <u>D</u>ay |
| 4. family relationships <u>with</u> names (Do NOT capitalize father, mother, sister, or brother, unless you're using those words as a name.) | <u>A</u>unt <u>B</u>ernice, <u>U</u>ncle <u>H</u>enry My <u>f</u>ather is a teacher. <u>I</u> will ask <u>M</u>other to drive. |
| 5. brand names | <u>R</u>ed <u>W</u>ing shoes, <u>F</u>ord trucks, <u>M</u>ountain <u>D</u>ew soda |
| 6. first words and important words in titles of books, poems, stories, plays, movies, songs, and so on | <u>W</u>ebster's <u>D</u>ictionary, <u>S</u>aturday <u>N</u>ight <u>L</u>ive |

7. nationalities, languages      Cherokee, English, Hispanic

8. people's names and initials,      Senator Thompson,
   including important words      R. L. Stine,
   in their titles      LeAnn Rimes,
        Mary, Queen of Scots,
        Vice President Al Gore

   _____

9. the first letter of each entry in      My Favorite Movie Stars
   an outline; BUT, follow standard
   capitalization rules for titles      A. Male actors
           1. Action heroes
             a. Bruce Willis
             b. Jackie Chan
           2._____

10. the salutation (greeting) in a letter      Dear Abby,
         Dear Mr. Rogers:

    • _____

    • _____

11. the first word of the complimentary      Your humble servant,
    closing in a letter      Igor

         Love,
         Jorge

    • _____

    • _____

12. North, South, East, West when      I like to vacation in the South.
    used as a geographic area      He lives on the West Coast.

    _____

    _____

13. all other proper nouns not      World War II, Dairy Queen,
    addressed here      United Airlines, Oval Office

    _____

# The Wise Guys

As you'll hear over and over again in this book, there are plenty of exceptions to every rule. Following are a few common exceptions to the capitalization rules.

| Do NOT capitalize: | Example: |
|---|---|
| 1. school courses, except languages | <u>a</u>rt, <u>h</u>istory, <u>g</u>eography; BUT <u>F</u>rench |
| 2. titles used after a name | Elizabeth II, the <u>q</u>ueen of England; BUT Queen Elizabeth II |
| 3. school years/grades | <u>s</u>ophomore, <u>f</u>reshman, <u>s</u>enior |
| 4. seasons | <u>s</u>pring, <u>s</u>ummer, <u>f</u>all, <u>w</u>inter |
| 5. words that were once proper nouns but have taken a general or generic meaning | <u>f</u>rench <u>f</u>ries, <u>c</u>hina dinnerware <u>t</u>rampoline |
| 6. articles or prepositions in titles unless appearing as the first word | *To Kill <u>a</u> Mockingbird* |

⚠ If you print your essays, be sure that your capitalized letters are larger than the other letters. You must make it clear to your audience which letters are capitalized.

## PRACTICE ACTIVITY

**Directions:** Rewrite the following sentences, capitalizing every letter necessary. If you need to, look back to the previous two pages for help.

1. many battles took place in new york during the revolutionary war.

_____

_____

2. dave's mother, the basketball referee, owns a lincoln continental sedan.

_____

_____

3. after hearing testimonies from both sides, judge albert questioned the truth of the smiths' allegation.

_____

_____

4. last weekend, my cousin ruth insisted that i try some carrot juice from health and happiness, a deli on main street.

_____

_____

5. how did your french test go last tuesday?

_____

6. carl perkins wrote "blue suede shoes," a song that elvis popularized.

_____

_____

7. ramona begged her parents to take her to niagara falls over spring vacation.

_____

_____

8. the teachers who assign the most reading are my english and american history teachers.

_____

_____

9. i think cassie would like the movie *titanic*.

_____

_____

10. my uncle tiny, who is huge, once played one of the mean stepsisters in a production of *cinderella*.

_____

_____

# Lesson 14: Commas

*Have you ever, noticed, when a sentence, is filled to overflowing, with commas, that are, unnecessary, you, begin to wonder, when, or if, the sentence, is ever, ever, going to end?*

A comma is simply a signal for your readers to pause before they go on. There are many rules about the use of commas, but the majority of situations are covered by the five rules that follow. Read the rules and examples, then add your own examples on the lines provided.

1. Use commas after items in a series. If you list three or more items in a row, put a comma after each item in the series except the last one. (Note that most newspapers and magazines ignore this rule. They do so to save space.)

   *Donald couldn't wait until Huey, Dewey, and Louie left.*

   *Clark spends his free time defending truth, justice, and the American way.*

   _____

   _____

## Set It Aside

Commas also have another useful purpose. They are often used to set apart the essential words in a sentence from the nonessential words. The next four rules will explain this more fully.

2. Use a comma after an introductory phrase. A **phrase** is a group of words without a subject and verb of its own. A short phrase that introduces the main idea of the sentence is called an **introductory phrase**. An introductory phrase is followed by a comma.

   *According to Pedro, the coaches have mentioned trying him as a first-string halfback.*

   *In the hours preceding the accident, Junior had felt a strange premonition.*

   _____

   _____

3. Use commas to set off appositives. An **appositive** is a group of words that describes a noun or a pronoun. It can occur at the beginning, middle, or end of a sentence. An appositive is set off by commas.

    *Patricia, a regular whiz at math, is working on improving her chess game.*

    *No one is sure how Tomasina mastered Super Mario Cart, a game that requires a lot of concentration.*

    _____

    _____

4. Use commas to set off parenthetical expressions. A **parenthetical expression** is a phrase that modifies the entire sentence. It is almost a side remark and is not needed for understanding the sentence. Parenthetical expressions are set off by commas. Some common parenthetical expressions are "as a matter of fact," "believe me," "I am sure," "to tell the truth," and "it seems to me."

    *My sister's new puppy is, to put it mildly, a non-stop chewing machine.*

    *Unless he joins the circus, which wouldn't surprise me, Aaron is likely to attend St. Francis College after he graduates from high school.*

    _____

    _____

5. Use commas to set off nonessential clauses. A **clause** is a group of words that has a subject and a verb of its own. There are two kinds of clauses: **essential** (or restrictive clauses) and **nonessential** (or nonrestrictive).

    *This is the video <u>that I want</u>.*　　　　　　　　*(essential)*

    *She sat alone, <u>far from all the others</u>*　　　　*(nonessential)*

An **essential clause** cannot be eliminated without changing the meaning of the sentence.

    *Go to the second house <u>that has a bay window</u>.*

If we remove the underlined clause, the meaning of the sentence changes. The speaker wants someone to go to fifty houses, if necessary, until that person reaches the second house with a bay window. The clause "that has a bay window" is essential to the correct meaning of the sentence.

A **nonessential clause** can be eliminated without changing the meaning of the sentence.

*Go to the second house, <u>which has a bay window</u>.*

If we remove the italicized clause, the meaning of the sentence does not change. The person will still go to the second house. The underlined clause is not essential to the correct meaning of the sentence.

Essential clauses are NOT set off with commas; nonessential clauses ARE set off with commas.

Now write a sentence that contains a clause. Use commas to set off the clause only if it is nonessential.

_____

_____

## Check, Please

This is just a partial list of the many uses of commas. You probably know that commas are used for dates, addresses, and a variety of other reasons. Those rules are usually pretty clear. The other rules will get easier with practice.

## PRACTICE ACTIVITY

**Directions:** Proofread the sentences below. Place a comma wherever one is needed. Each of the following sentences will need at least one comma.

1. If we arrive late believe me everyone else will have started to eat.

2. Being prone to snags John brought extra fishing line sinkers and hooks with him.

3. Always one of the first to understand a lesson Lindsay often helped the teacher explain it to the others.

4. Carrie named the seven piglets Dopey Doc Grumpy Happy Sleepy Bashful and Ralph.

5. In typical fashion Mark blabbed the secret to everyone he knew.

6. The secret to success she knew lay in gaining people's confidence.

7. Hendrix Clapton Page and Walsh were the best guitarists of that era.

8. Elmer an expert carpenter often criticizes the quality of lumber available in his area.

9. The coach has arranged for us to scrimmage West Liberty the second-best team in the league.

10. Each computer is equipped with a color monitor a CD drive and a modem.

# Lesson 15: End Punctuation

*Do you know what's going on here!*

*Yippee. Isn't it great to be alive.*

*Darling, I love you?*

The easiest part of punctuating a sentence may be finding the right mark of end punctuation. Your only choices are a period, a question mark, or an exclamation point. Read the following rules and examples, then add your own examples on the lines provided.

1. Use a question mark to show that someone is asking a question.

    *Can you come with me and my family to the cabin this weekend?*

⚠ Do NOT use a question mark when you are talking about someone asking a question.

*Jennifer asked her cousin if he could come with her and her family to the cabin this weekend.*

_____

_____

2. Use an exclamation point to show great emotion following an interjection (*Wow! Terrific!* etc.) or at the end of a sentence.

    *No! No way, no how, not ever!*

_____

_____

3. If a sentence could be read either way, use a period. Sometimes deciding between an exclamation point and a period is a tough call. Trust your instincts. If the sentence seems to express strong emotion, go for the exclamation point. If not, you're probably safest to go for the period.

   *Absolutely! No problem!*

   *Absolutely. No problem.*

   *No. I don't think so.*

   _____

   _____

4. Use a period to end a statement that does NOT show great emotion or ask a question.

   *Thomas Alva Edison was known as "The Wizard of Menlo Park."*

   *The judge ruled that there was insufficient evidence to try the case.*

   _____

   _____

## PRACTICE ACTIVITY

**Directions:** Proofread the sentences below. Place a period, question mark, or exclamation point in the blank at the end of each sentence or interjection. Each sentence needs ending punctuation.

1. Stop that_____

2. Trudy asked her little brother Rudy if the Oilers had won their game against the Cowboys_____

3. Robin, where'd we park the Batmobile_____

4. Boris likes to sit in front of the television for hours, flipping from one channel to the next_____

5. Remember to turn out all the lights when you leave_____

6. Did you know that Kelly got straight A's, sang in choir, tutored disadvantaged youth, and lettered in volleyball her freshman year_____

7. Karen asked Todd, "Can you figure out the answer to the second problem_____"

8. I thought the movie could have used a few more explosions and car chases_____

9. OUCH_____

10. I made this pie especially for you: Enjoy_____

# Lesson 16: Affixed Words

*"I guess it's perfectly understandable that I should have a predisposition for correctly spelling affixed words," Clive said. "My parents are from the English towns of Suffix and Prefix."*

Many words in the English language are made up of smaller parts. These parts include a base word (sometimes called a **root** word), and affixes (a **prefix,** or a **suffix,** or both). While this workbook can't teach you to spell every affixed word in the English language, it will provide you with the most basic rules you need to know and some practice exercises to get you started.

In addition to spelling affixed words, it's also a good idea to become familiar with the way an affix changes a base word's meaning. This chapter will take a look at some of the most common prefixes and suffixes and their meanings.

1. In the paragraph about Clive at the top of this page, underline each affixed word.

# A Prefix Comes First

A **prefix** is a word part that is added to the beginning of a base word in order to change its meaning. The table below shows some common prefixes and their meanings.

| Prefix | Meaning | Examples |
|--------|---------|----------|
| *anti-* | against, preventing, the opposite of, false | antibiotic<br>antiseptic<br>antifreeze<br>antihero |
| *dis-* | the opposite of, not | disappear<br>disintegrate<br>disagree<br>dissimilar |
| *il-* | against, not | illegal<br>illegible |
| *im-* | not | immobile<br>impractical<br>immortal |
| *in-* | the opposite of, not | inefficient<br>incompetent<br>incapable |
| *mis-* | badly, wrong, not | misunderstood<br>misbehave<br>misplace |
| *pre-* | in front of, prior to (before) | prefix<br>preshrunk<br>predetermine |
| *over-* | beyond, more than | overdue<br>overspent<br>oversight |
| *un-* | the opposite of, not | unfair<br>unhappy |
| *under-* | less than, not enough, beneath | underpaid<br>underfed<br>underwear |

# The Rule for Adding a Prefix

Attaching a prefix to a base word is like linking two boxcars on a train. Nothing changes, they just get hooked together. For example, look at the list below.

2. Write in your own examples on the lines provided.

| Prefix | Base Word | Affixed Word |
| --- | --- | --- |
| anti- | freeze | antifreeze |
| il- | logical | illogical |
| im- | material | immaterial |
| in- | effective | ineffective |
| pre- | view | preview |
| un- | like | unlike |
| under- | ground | underground |

# At the End of It All

A **suffix** is a word part that is added to the end of a base word in order to change its meaning or the way it can be used.

3. Write your own examples on the lines provided.

| Suffix | Meaning | Example |
|--------|---------|---------|
| -able | able to be or become something, worthy of being or becoming something | perishable<br>comparable<br>trainable<br>admirable<br><br>_____ |
| -al | suitable for, of, or like, relating to | approval<br>removal<br><br>_____ |
| -en | make, become, made of | strengthen<br>brighten<br>wooden<br><br>_____ |
| -ize | make, become, cause to be | traumatize<br>dramatize<br>legalize<br><br>_____ |
| -ity | the state of being something, having the character of being a certain way or thing | possibility<br>tranquility<br><br>_____ |
| -less | without or lacking something | fearless<br>tireless<br>careless<br>pitiless<br><br>_____ |
| -ly | in such a manner, like or suited to, occuring every so often | swiftly<br>perfectly<br>truly<br>earthly<br>hourly<br>yearly<br><br>_____ |
| -ness | the state of being something | kindness<br>sweetness<br><br>_____ |

Adding a suffix to a base word may or may not change its spelling. The quickest way to increase your chances of knowing whether or not a change occurs in the base word is to learn the following rules.

Read the rules and examples, then write your own examples on the lines provided.

1.  Do not change the base word when adding a suffix that begins with a consonant, unless the base word ends in *y*.

    | | | |
    |---|---|---|
    | *clear* | *-ly* | *clearly* |
    | *eager* | *-ness* | *eagerness* |
    | *care* | *-less* | _____ |

2.  In general, if a base word ends in a *y*, change the *y* to an *i* before adding a suffix.

    | | | |
    |---|---|---|
    | *study* | *-ous* | *studious* |
    | *silly* | *-ness* | *silliness* |
    | *glory* | *-fy* | _____ |

    If the suffix begins with an *i*, however, do <u>not</u> change the *y*.

    | | | |
    |---|---|---|
    | *try* | *-ing* | *trying* |

    ⚠ Watch for the following exception:

    | | | |
    |---|---|---|
    | *harmony* | *-ize* | *harmonize* |
    | *play* | *-ing* | _____ |

3.  If the base word ends in an *e* and the suffix begins with a vowel, drop the final *e*.

    | | | |
    |---|---|---|
    | *shine* | *-ing* | *shining* |
    | *desire* | *-able* | *desirable* |
    | *dance* | *-er* | *dancer* |
    | *grease* | *-y* | *greasy* |
    | *remove* | *-al* | _____ |

4.  If the base word ends in *e* and the suffix begins with a consonant, keep the final *e*.

    | | | |
    |---|---|---|
    | *move* | *-ment* | *movement* |
    | *hope* | *-ful* | *hopeful* |
    | *grace* | *-ful* | _____ |

⚠ Watch for the following exceptions:

| | | |
|---|---|---|
| *true* | *-ly* | *truly* |
| *whole* | *-ly* | *wholly* |

5. Probably the most difficult decision for most people is when to double the final consonant of the base word. Double the final consonant only when the following conditions are present:

- The base word ends in a consonant with only one vowel in front of it, the suffix begins in a vowel,

   AND

   the word has only one syllable, or the accent of the spoken word is on the <u>final</u> syllable.

- The word has only one syllable.

| | | |
|---|---|---|
| *clap* | *-ing* | *clapping* |
| *win* | *-er* | *winner* |
| *thin* | *-er* | _____ |

- The word has the accent on the last syllable.

| | | |
|---|---|---|
| *refer* | *-al* | *referral* |
| *admit* | *-ance* | *admittance* |
| *permit* | *-ed* | _____ |

⚠ Watch for the following exceptions:

| | | |
|---|---|---|
| *remember* | *-ing* | *remembering* |
| *greed* | *-y* | *greedy* |

## PRACTICE ACTIVITY

**Directions:** In the following exercise, join the word parts to make affixed words on the lines provided.

| Prefix | Base Word | Suffix | Affixed Word |
|--------|-----------|--------|--------------|
| inter- | nation | -al | 1. _____ |
| | sing | -ing | 2. _____ |
| un- | luck | -y | 3. _____ |
| | glory | -ous | 4. _____ |
| | happy | -ness | 5. _____ |
| pre- | judge | | 6. _____ |
| il- | logic | -al | 7. _____ |
| pre- | dispose | -ed | 8. _____ |
| dis- | satisfy | -ed | 9. _____ |
| | plan | -ing | 10. _____ |
| under- | sell | | 11. _____ |
| over- | ride | -ing | 12. _____ |
| inter- | rupt | | 13. _____ |
| | diverse | -ity | 14. _____ |
| post- | script | | 15. _____ |
| non- | conform | -ity | 16. _____ |
| | terror | -ize | 17. _____ |
| dis- | guise | -ed | 18. _____ |

# Lesson 17: Contractions

*"Isn't it time to surrender the starship to the Voracian Warbird?" Lieutenant Analog asked. "We can't sacrifice the crew for a losing battle. And you know we can't win. We don't have a chance with our shields down."*

*"Security!" the Captain shouted. "Arrest this man. This is not Lieutenant Analog. It could only be his evil android twin, Bobulac 2."*

*"You're wrong, Captain," the android insisted. "It's me, Analog. You're making a terrible mistake."*

*"I'm afraid not, Bob," the Captain said. "Lieutenant Analog never uses contractions. He's not programmed to use them as you are."*

Most people use contractions all the time, especially when speaking. As a matter of fact, it would sound almost unnatural if they didn't, just as it sounded unnatural when the Captain heard his favorite android use them. For example, what if you said, "Would it not be nice if we got out of school early today?" Your friends would probably think that you were trying to be funny, or that you had been replaced by an android.

To use contractions effectively in your writing, you have to be able to form them correctly. Writers often use contractions to give their work a more informal, conversational tone. Contractions serve to reflect the way we speak.

## What's a Contraction, Anyway?

A **contraction** is a new word that is formed by joining two other words together in a special way. Some of the letters of one word have been left out, and in their place is an apostrophe (').

The trick of correctly forming contractions is knowing which letters to leave out of which word and where to place the apostrophe. Since there actually are very few contractions in the English language, your best bet is to learn them by heart.

**Contractions fall into groups that share certain characteristics.**

If you think of contractions as belonging to "families," you might find learning to spell them fairly easy. The following exercise works with contraction word families. Read the examples, them fill in the missing pieces of the table.

| Word Family | Two words | Resulting contraction | What's missing |
|---|---|---|---|
| *am* | I am | I'm | *a* from "am" |
| *are* | you are<br>1. _____ | you're<br>we're | *a* from "are" |
| *is* | he is<br>it is<br>she is<br>2. _____<br>3. _____<br>what is<br>who is | he's<br>it's<br>4. _____<br>that's<br>there's<br>5. _____<br>6. _____ | *i* from "is" |
| *have* | I have<br>they have<br>7. _____ | I've<br>8. _____<br>we've | *ha* from "have" |
| *not* | are not<br>9. _____<br>do not<br>10. _____<br>had not<br>11. _____<br>12. _____<br>is not<br>might not<br>13. _____<br>14. _____<br>were not<br>would not | aren't<br>couldn't<br>15. _____<br>doesn't<br>16. _____<br>hasn't<br>haven't<br>17. _____<br>18. _____<br>shouldn't<br>wasn't<br>19. _____<br>20. _____ | *o* from "not" |
| *will* | he will<br>I will<br>it will<br>21. _____<br>that will<br>there will<br>22. _____<br>we will | he'll<br>23. _____<br>24. _____<br>she'll<br>25. _____<br>26. _____<br>they'll<br>27. _____ | *wi* from "will" |
| *would* | he would<br>I would<br>she would<br>28. _____<br>we would | he'd<br>29. _____<br>30. _____<br>they'd<br>31. _____ | *woul* from "would" |

# Be On the Lookout for Renegades

As with nearly every other rule you've learned in this book, there are exceptions to the contraction rules.

**Learn to spell contractions that don't follow the rules. It's the only way to get them right on the test.**

Following are two common characters that can't, or won't, behave themselves.

| The words: | Their contractions: |
|---|---|
| *will not* | *won't* |
| *can not* | *can't* |

**It's is not the same as its.**

A lot of people have trouble using "its" and "it's" in the right places. For an example of correct usage, look at the following sentences:

*Someone in town is selling a 1965 Mustang; <u>it's</u> listed in the paper for $4,000. I wonder what <u>its</u> condition is. Maybe I'll get my older brother to call the number, just for kicks.*

In the first sentence, the word *it's* is a contraction of the phrase "it is." The apostrophe tells us that one or more letters have been removed in forming a single word out of two.

The word *its*, without the apostrophe, indicates a possessive. In the second sentence, the speaker refers to the condition of the car as "*its* condition." Similarly, one might refer to its engine, its color, or its upholstery.

This spelling for the possessive of *it* may be confusing at first, since most possessives are formed using an "apostrophe + *s*." But it's simply the rule. If in doubt whether to use *its* or *it's*, try substituting "it is." If "it is" makes sense, use an apostrophe. Otherwise, don't.

In other words, you wouldn't say "I like the car's body style and *it is* color." So you wouldn't write, "I like the car's body style and *it's* color." The word you are looking for is the possessive form of *it*: *its*.

## PRACTICE ACTIVITY

**Directions**: Identify the contraction that is formed CORRECTLY.

1. A. hadnt'
   B. she'is
   C. h'ed
   D. what's

2. A. we've
   B. shoul'dnt
   C. she'l
   D. cann't

3. A. does'nt
   B. won't
   C. wer'e
   D. Im

4. A. might'nt
   B. we'd
   C. wern't
   D. who'is

5. A. 'Id
   B. there'r
   C. is'nt
   D. they've

6. A. that'd
   B. arent'
   C. thatl'l
   D. theres'

7. A. woudn't
   B. w'ed
   C. the'yre
   D. don't

# Appendix

## Answer Explanations

Below and on the following pages are detailed explanations for the multiple choice Sample Questions appearing at the end of Lessons 1 through 9.

### Lesson 1: Main Idea and Theme

#### The Panther and the Heron, page 12

1. C  Courage (A), jealousy (B), and physical pain (D) all play a part in this story, but the focus of the selection is on how Panther's selfishness causes him to lose his friendship with Heron.

2. D  Panther doesn't appreciate the kind deed done by Heron, and he ends up being worse off because of it. Choice D most clearly echoes this theme. It means, "don't turn against someone who helps you."

3. A  Choices B, C, and D are all events that happen at some point in the story. The best summary, however, is one that includes the two central events: Heron helps Panther; Panther makes Heron a promise but breaks it later.

4. C  This scene shows Panther turning on the friend who has helped him. Not only does Panther not help Heron, but he also threatens Heron by snapping his jaws at him. This makes it clear that Panther is a bully.

## Lesson 2: Details and Sequencing of Events

### The Martians Have Landed!, page 20

1. C  This detail is mentioned in paragraph 2.

2. C  Choices A, B, and D are all mentioned at some point in the selection. Nothing is said, however, about anyone being killed in the panic.

3. A  In paragraph 10, the author directly links the threat of war in Europe to the nervousness of Americans. The other choices are all details mentioned in the selection, but the author never suggests they were reasons for the uneasiness in America in 1938.

4. C  The selection says that the hurricane (D) struck before the broadcast of *War of the Worlds* (B). The lawsuits (A) were filed immediately after the broadcast. Orson Welles left radio only after the Mercury Theatre of the Air became successful (C). This event clearly happened after the rest of the events listed.

## Lesson 3: Vocabulary in Context

### Rachel Carson, page 30

1. B  From the context, it is clear that Rachel Carson has an idea of what is going wrong with the wildlife around her and wants to find out whether she's right. The only answer choice that fits this meaning is *prove*.

2. D  The paragraph describes the *avid* bird watcher as someone who had done "intensive observation" of birds. Only *dedicated* matches this description.

3. C  Putting the word in quotation marks suggests that this is a label other people use that the author may not agree with. The answer that comes closest to this is C. Choice A may seem attractive; however, the adjective *bad* is being used to describe insects other than mosquitoes.

4. A  The sentence says Carson wanted to "verify" her hunch. Since we know *verify* means "prove," we can say a hunch is some sort of unproved assumption. The next paragraph describes the evidence behind Carson's hunch. Clearly her hunch is not based on mistakes (D). It is best described as an "educated guess." Choices B and C do not fit the context of the selection.

5. B  From the context, it's clear that *ominous* means the opposite of fairy tale, the term used to describe the very beginning of Carson's book. The most likely choices would seem to be *scary* (B) or *violent* (C). But nothing violent is described in the quotation from Carson's book, there's only the threat that something horrible is beginning to happen. Scary is the best choice.

6.  D   The last paragraph describes how the use of chemicals changed after Rachel Carson's book was published. The author suggests these actions were directly caused by Carson's book, not simply that Carson had wished for them (B). This suggests that Carson's *legacy* was the *contribution* she made to the safer use of chemicals in nature. Choices A and C do not fit the context of the selection.

## Lesson 4: Visual Information Sources

### How to Make Cut Flowers Last, page 41

1.  C   A vase is mentioned only in these three steps.

2.  D   Step 2 states that the instrument must be sharp. The items listed in choices A through C are either too dull or too unwieldy to use.

3.  C   See Step 4.

### Map, page 42

4.  D   The Public Library (A) is on the corner of Center and Taft, as is the Post Office (B). The Courthouse (C) is located on the northeast corner of Center and Court.

5.  B   The only exit from the parking lot of the museum is on Wright Blvd.; eliminate choices A and D. It is not possible to travel west on Rutherford from Wright Blvd. (C).

6.  A   Taft does not intersect with I-25 (B). Choices C and D are both located in sector A3.

### Faculty Table, page 43

7.  B   The only column that is in any order is "Books Written," which ranges from 2 to 9.

8.  D   Dexter has been on the faculty for 23 years.

### Why People Don't Vote, page 43

9.  A   The third largest "piece of the pie" is labeled "Do not like candidates."

10.  C   The survey is of nonvoters.

## Lesson 5: Inference and Conclusion

### The Moustache, pages 52 and 53

1.  B   Their relationship is certainly not tense (A). Nor can it be described as humorous (D). Although the answer might be (C) carefree, meaning relaxed, the most accurate description is friendly (B).

2.  A   There is nothing in the passage to indicate that B, C, or D is correct. Mike's mother does say, frowning: "That hair. Well, at least you combed it," implying that she does not like the style.

3.  C   There is nothing in the passage to make the reader infer that A or D could be correct. Mike is not wearing a moustache *because* his mother doesn't like it (B); his mother doesn't like it because he *is* wearing it. Choice C is the correct response. Mike is wearing a moustache simply because he likes it and thinks it looks good on him.

4. A  This response can be inferred from paragraph 9, which explains that the box office attendant "took one look at my moustache and charged me full price."

5. D  The correct answer is found at paragraph 11, in which Mike says, " 'Look,' I said, to cheer her up. 'I'm thinking about shaving it off.' Even though I wasn't."

## Lesson 6: Logical Relationships

### To Build a Fire, page 62

1. B  Paragraph 4 states that the man had received advice from an old-timer at Sulphur Creek.

2. C  Paragraph 7 describes how hard it is for the man to get his shoelaces off, then says he decides to draw the knife. Paragraph 8 begins with the phrase, "But before he could cut the strings . . .". This clearly suggests that he drew out the knife to cut his laces.

3. D  The last paragraph says that the fire was put out by snow that came from the tree branches above the fire, not an avalanche (C) or the tree itself falling on the fire (B). The same paragraph specifically says the wind had not been blowing (A), and that it was because of the still air that the snow had built up on the tree branches.

4. B  Paragraph 3 says that the man knew the only way to save himself once he got his feet wet was to build a fire. The selection never says anything to contradict this belief.

## Lesson 7: Author's Purpose and Viewpoint

### If You Win, I Lose? Get Lost! and What Have You Got to Lose?, pages 72 and 73

1. C  The author does not strongly protest all sporting activities (A). She does, however, amuse readers with incidents from her childhood (D) and make fun of those who are not athletic (B), particularly herself. But her *main* purpose is to describe the negative effects of competition in a humorous way (C).

2. A  In paragraph 1, the author jokingly ridicules herself. She calls herself a klutz, then goes on to give several examples of her klutziness.

3. B  The author does not stress the importance of athletic skills (A), encourage all students to compete in track (C), or try to gain recognition for her achievements in athletics (D).

4. B  The primary purpose of paragraph 1 is to provide the reader a perspective for the author's views about athletic competition.

5. A  Although the author is not furious (B), she is critical (A) of competitive sports, especially for young people. Her tone is critical toward competition, not satisfied (C) or resigned (D).

6. D  The author attempts to motivate and encourage students to participate in competitive sports.

7. B  The correct answer is B. The author's attitude toward her rivals is competitive in a positive, friendly way. A, C, and D are all negative. Only B is true to the position the author takes in the paragraph. In the last sentence, she says that her rivals' victories challenged her to work harder, a very positive way of looking at the situation.

8. C  Because these selections are opinion pieces, they are most likely to be found in an editorial section of some publication.

## Lesson 8: Story Elements

### Starship to Sirius, page 85

1. **A** The focus of the selection is on Toby's struggle with his own doubts about himself and his new home. It's clear he has a close relationship with his mother and loved his grandfather (B, C). The captain of the Pegasus is not mentioned in the story (D).

2. **B** The author describes Toby's mother as "glowing" when she is talking to him about their arrival at Danae. She says that it's "amazing" that they're almost there. This strongly suggests that she's excited about arriving at Danae.

3. **A** The selection ends with Toby questioning whether he will do well in his new home without Grandfather to guide him. It is likely that the rest of the story will answer that question. The events mentioned in the other choices are not likely to surpass the theme described in choice A.

4. **C** Because the selection focuses on Toby's feelings, it is these feelings that determine the overall mood of the selection. Toby is certainly not joyful (A) or happy (D) about arriving at Danae. He's worried about how things will go when they reach their new home. But the selection doesn't say he was actually fearful about their arrival either (B). Toby has mixed feelings as he thinks about his future home. He's *concerned* about his ability to deal with his new surroundings.

5. **C** The selection does not exhibit the characteristics of a folk tale (A). It tells a story about fictional characters; eliminate choice B. It also seems to be set in the future (although no specific date is given); eliminate choice D. Even more important, the story revolves around scientific technology (gigantic starships, colonizing new planets, etc.). The selection is best described as science fiction.

## Lesson 9: Poetry Elements

### Runaway Train, page 94

1. **C** The "runaway train" is not an actual train (A, B); it is invisible, doesn't run on coal, and doesn't require a ticket. The "train" is transporting runaway slaves (C), not coal (D).

2. **B** The system used to help runaway slaves escape to the north is called the Underground Railroad. The "trains" running on this railroad are not real; they are groups of people guided by conductors such as Harriet Tubman. The poet is speaking metaphorically. This metaphor is drawn upon throughout the poem. The poem does not use the words *like* or *as* to compare this system to a train; the comparison is much stronger than a simile (A). Exaggeration (C) and (D) personification are not used in the poem.

3. **C** See the first and second lines of the second stanza.

4. **A** The train is kept secret so that the escaped slaves and their "conductors" are not caught. The poem does not support choices B, C, or D.

5. **B** Strangers worked together on the underground railroad to help runaway slaves escape from the South to the North.

# New York Learning Standards for English Language Arts

*Sharpen Up on New York English Language Arts, Book 8,* is based on the learning standards tested by the New York State Testing Program.

| Standard | Description |
|---|---|
| 1 | **Language for Information and Understanding** |
| | 1. **Listening and reading** to acquire information and understanding involves collecting data, facts, and ideas; discovering relationships, concepts, and generalizations; and using knowledge from oral, written, and electronic sources. |
| | 2. **Speaking and writing** to acquire and transmit information requires asking probing and clarifying questions, interpreting information from one's own words, applying information from one context to another, and presenting the information and interpretation clearly, concisely, and comprehensibly. |
| 2 | **Language for Literary Response and Expression** |
| | 1. **Listening and reading** for literary response involves comprehending, interpreting, and critiquing imaginative texts in every medium, drawing on personal experiences and knowledge to understand the text, and recognizing the social, historical, and cultural features of the text. |
| | 2. **Speaking and writing** for literary response involves presenting interpretations, analyses, and reactions to the content and language of a text. Speaking and writing for literary expression involves producing imaginative texts that use language and text structures that are inventive and often multilayered. |
| 3 | **Language for Critical Analysis and Evaluation** |
| | 1. **Listening and reading** to analyze and evaluate experiences, ideas, information, and issues requires using evaluative criteria from a variety of perspectives and recognizing the difference in evaluations based on different sets of criteria. |
| | 2. **Speaking and writing** for critical analysis and evaluation requires presenting opinions and judgments on experiences, ideas, information, and issues clearly, logically, and persuasively with reference to specific criteria on which the opinion or judgment is based. |